Ernest Rhys, Arthur Hugh Clough

The Bothie, and Other Poems

By Arthur Hugh Clough

Ernest Rhys, Arthur Hugh Clough

The Bothie, and Other Poems
By Arthur Hugh Clough

ISBN/EAN: 9783337370114

Printed in Europe, USA, Canada, Australia, Japan

Cover: Foto ©Thomas Meinert / pixelio.de

More available books at **www.hansebooks.com**

THE BOTHIE, AND OTHER POEMS: BY ARTHUR HUGH CLOUGH

EDITED BY ERNEST RHYS

LONDON

WALTER SCOTT, LIMITED

PATERNOSTER SQUARE

NEW YORK: 3 EAST FOURTEENTH STREET

CONTENTS.

CONTENTS.

INTRODUCTION.

THE favourite pupil of Dr. Arnold, the disciple of Wordsworth, the friend of Emerson, Clough was a true child of his time, and his poems count among its most intimate documents. The only one of his longer poems that has gained the ear of the world, " The Bothie," appeared as early as 1848, in the mid-century; but intellectually he was in advance of his day, and it is only now, late in the century, that he is gaining full audience for his whole performance, brief as it is.

His grave lies in Florence, near the graves of Mrs. Barrett Browning and Landor, in the little Protestant cemetery. He died there, at the early age of forty-three. He was born at Liverpool on the first day of 1819, and he travelled far in more senses than one, on his way from the Mersey to the Arno. He went to America twice, once as a child of four, and again as a man of thirty-four. He knew the Welsh mountains and the Scottish Highlands, as well as the London streets; the Concord of Emerson and the Harvard Cambridge, as well as the English Rugby and Oxford. If his accent is Oxford, then, it is an Oxford with a difference; and his message is modern, and his attitude without prejudice.

He came of mixed race. Wales and Yorkshire were in his blood; still more remotely there was a Dutch ancestress. His father's family had been settled for three centuries and more at Plâs-Clough, in Denbigh, dating from a Sir Richard Clough, who built the house about 1527. In the eighteenth century there was a Hugh Clough, a friend of the poet Cowper and somewhat given to poetry himself, who was a Fellow of King's College, Cambridge, and lies buried there. This may serve to show a comfortable tradition of culture and country ease in the family; but the present poet's father broke the tradition on one side by leaving the Welsh family seat and entering upon a life of commerce at Liverpool, and afterwards at Charles-town, in Virginia, not altogether successfully. In fact, his business embarrassments were such as to affect crucially his most famous son's future, and to add considerably to its burden of life.

Meanwhile, the boy was gaining early impressions of America at Charlestown, where one hears of him reading " Captain Cook's Travels " among his father's cotton-bales, and listening to the sea-tales of the ship captains who visited his father's house,—" a large, ugly red-brick house near the sea." "Its lower storey," says his sister, who describes these early days, "was my father's office, and it was close by a wharf where from our windows we could see the vessels lying by, and amuse ourselves with watching their movements."

In June 1828 the family returned to England on a brief visit, and Arthur was sent to school at Chester, with an elder brother, Charles ; and so, in the following year to Rugby. Here, the influence of Dr. Arnold told most powerfully upon him from the first. The boy's father and mother had gone back to Charlestown, and Dr. Arnold, according to his wont, became a second father to this brilliant pupil. His holidays passed in various parts of North Wales, or in Yorkshire, in the houses of various

a *

family connections, well-to-do vicars and the like, who are revived for us and most perfectly represented in the pleasant rhymes of *Primitiæ*, the first tale told in his last and maturest poem—" Mari Magno." But all through his Rugby days, whether term time or holiday, he seems to have worked harder than goes with health and a boy's happiness. There was always a certain strain upon him ; he wanted rest, we are told ; and again, " he was much exhausted by the intense interest and labour he expended on his moral work among the boys, and also on the *Rugby Magazine*." Physically, too, he purchased a similar distinction, at as heavy cost. He was " the best goal-keeper on record ; " and " one of the first swimmers in the school,"—a boyish leader in everything ; but he paid in nervous energy for his lead.

It was the same at Oxford, where he proceeded in 1837, having gained the Balliol Scholarship during the year preceding. He was not content with the regular undergraduate's interests, intellectual and what not ; but must needs encounter all that fierce theology, and its controversies, to be found in the Oxford of the Tractarian movement, with Dr. Newman, eloquent and inevitable, in its midst. A premature forcing it proved for Clough, followed by a corresponding reaction. "His intellectual perplexity," says Mr. Ward, "preyed heavily on his spirits and grievously interfered with his studies."

He read hard, and lived hard, notwithstanding. "He had," says Mrs. Clough, "very cold rooms in Balliol, on the ground-floor, in which he passed a whole winter without a fire ; and he used to say that this was an excellent plan for keeping out visitors, as nobody else could stand it for more than a few minutes." He failed afterwards in getting his "first," which severely disappointed Dr. Arnold and his own people ; and he failed to get the Balliol Fellowship, for which he tried ; but in 1842 he was elected Fellow of Oriel. These failures and successes, with the test they supplied of the good opinion of the world, may have helped to teach him some of that fine half-cynical, half-kindly contempt for the conventional estimate of things which one finds in "Dipsychus" and so many of his other poems.

Dr. Arnold died in the same year as Clough

gained his fellowship, and the death was a great blow to him, for Arnold had done almost everything for him. He seemed completely stunned by it, his sister tells us. He went home to Liverpool from Oxford, on hearing the news; and then wandered off alone into the Welsh hills. Many of the poems in the little volume, *Ambarvalia*, appear to have been written in this and the following year, when he became a tutor, as well as a fellow, at Oriel. He kept the tutorship till 1848, at some sacrifice of his scruples on the old grounds of his disagreement with the orthodox belief. The terrible potato famine in Ireland led to his writing in 1847 a pamphlet on Retrenchment at Oxford, which is full of characteristic passages; for example:

"O ye, born to be rich, or at least born not to be poor; ye young men of Oxford, who gallop your horses over Bullingdon, and ventilate your fopperies arm-in-arm up the High Street, abuse if you will to the full that other plea of the spirits and the thoughtlessness of youth, but let me advise you to hesitate ere you venture the question, May I not do as I like with my own? ere you meddle with such edge tools as the subject of property. Some one, I fear, might be found to look up your title-deeds, and to quote inconvenient Scriptures."

The beginning of the new economics, indeed, is to be read between the lines of this pamphlet ; and the beginning of that movement which has led a later generation of Oxford in the steps of Arnold Toynbee.

Meanwhile, in 1847 and 1848, he was collecting in Scotland, during the long vacations with their reading parties, the impressions out of which "The Bothie" grew. We find him writing from Drumnadrochet, in July 1847 :—

"Yesterday I went to Foyers. It is by far the highest of the Scotch waterfalls, and there is a pleasant quiet sabbatic country-inn, overlooking the whole lake, with our highest hill, Mealfourvonie, just over the water, and with the Foyers river less than a mile off." In October he writes to the late Principal Shairp, who had often been a companion in such mountain rambles in the past, referring to the delights of the "Hesperian seclusion" he had been enjoying in the Highlands : "Woe's me," he adds, "but one doesn't like going back to Oxford, nor coming to Liverpool either ; no, nor seeing the face of hat-and-coat-wearing man, nor even of elegantly-attired woman."

In the following May he is in Paris,—"pottering about under the Tuileries chestnuts, and here and there about bridges and streets, *pour savourer la république.*" He describes very gaily and humorously the fête of May 22nd, and its procession :—

"The *jeunes filles* looked pretty in their white dresses, with the tricolour streaming from the left shoulder, and artificial oak-wreaths in their hair ; pretty *en masse*, but individually not remarkable either for face or figure. Moreover, they were declassicised by their use of parasols. . . . It was funny in the afternoon to see the classical virgins walking about with their papas and mamas, people of the under-shoe-making and back-street shop-keeping class. A good many of them were, about 6 P.M., dancing vigorously (without music) with *gardes mobiles* and other indiscriminates."

After Oxford, Paris : it was a change after his own heart, since he wished to live, and to see life, as well as to think and write. And he did not, as the last passage quoted might seem to suggest,

look at it only for its picturesque side. He saw it
through his own ethical medium, and weighed its
effects upon the future of England and Europe
with all seriousness. The end of the same letter
which sums up his Paris impressions announces
the advent of Emerson, whom he found much less
Emersonian than his Essays, and " very Yankee to
look at, lank and sallow, and not quite without the
twang ; but his looks and voice are pleasing nevertheless, and give you the impression of perfect
intellectual cultivation." This was written in July
1848; and in February 1849 he writes to Emerson
himself a very interesting letter, referring mainly to
"The Bothie," which he had been writing in the
interim.

"Will you convey to Mr. Longfellow," he writes,
"the fact that it was a reading of his ' Evangeline '
aloud to my mother and sister, which, coming after
a reperusal of the ' Iliad,' occasioned this outbreak
of hexameters ? "

As to its first reception by the British public,
he says : " Meantime, in England I shall not be
troubled with a very onerous weight of celebrity.
Mr. Kingsley, a chief writer in ' Fraser,' devoted

the whole of a cordial eulogistic article to the
'Pastoral,' and has made it tolerably known; but
the *Spectator* was contemptuous ; and in Oxford,
though there has been a fair sale and much talk of
it, the verdict is, that it is 'indecent and profane,
immoral and communistic !'"

"The Bothie," as originally published, in the
edition from which the present text is taken, was
an original-looking volume, in imperial octavo ;
which at a first glance reminds one in *format* of
the first edition of Walt Whitman's "Leaves of
Grass." A brief "note," on the back of the title-
page, gives the cue of Clough's laxity in the use of
the hexameter : "The reader is warned to expect
every kind of irregularity in these modern hexameters : spondaic lines, so called, are almost the
rule ; and a word will often require to be transposed
by the voice from the end of one line to the beginning of the next." In gauging the hexa-
metrical effect of "The Bothie," it is interesting
to know that Clough afterwards, in his "Letters
of Parepidemus," arrived at a humorous half-
condemnation of the attempt to use the form
modernly. "It is too late a day," he says, "to

introduce a new principle, however good, into modern European verse." He adds, in a rhymed conclusion :

"Could they but jingle a little, 'twere better, perhaps;
     but the trouble
Really is endless, of hunting for rhymes that have all to
     be double."

"The Bothie," we may add, was dedicated to "My Long-Vacation Pupils," as a "fiction, purely fiction."

"Ambarvalia," the second of Clough's books, to which he contributed the first half,—the second being the work of Thomas Burbidge, an old school-fellow, and fellow-contributor to the *Rugby Magazine*,—appeared in 1849. It was a very plain little volume, in depressing black covers,—very unlike the too-resplendent garb in which our minor poets of to-day mostly appear. After carefully reading Burbidge's half of the book, I have failed to discover any qualities in it sufficient to account for its association with Clough. Two sonnets only, one on London, another on "The Naming of the Stars," and a few felicitous lines, are all that are likely to take the ear and be remembered, as a sign that Burbidge, too, had his possibilities. Both the authors strike one in its pages rather as thinkers using verse as a medium, than poets using their art because they must; but Clough really had ideas and strong emotions, while Burbidge had only sentiments and grave considerations. Clough had at least a born gift of words; the other had only an acquired use of them.

Having carried the story in brief of Clough's career to the point of the publishing of his first two volumes,—the only two which come within the scope of the present selection; our record might be considered properly to cease. But one may be permitted to complete the tale in outline at least, if only to show how his earlier works bear upon his later ones.

In October 1849, true to his function of "Teacher," which he always considered his one predestinate rôle, he became the "Head" of University Hall, Gordon Square, London,—a building now partly occupied by Dr. Williams' Library. The main part of the year, prior to this, he spent abroad; and saw the siege of Rome by the French, and gathered

other interesting and stirring impressions of history,
ancient and modern. These are woven character-
istically into his second long poem, "Amours de
Voyage," also written in familiar hexameters,
whose title, remembering Clough's idiosyncrasy of
mind and temperament, may suggest its character.
In 1850 he went abroad again; and as Rome
colours "Amours de Voyage," Venice colours his
third longer work, "Dipsychus," one of the most
subtle and unconventional of modern poems, which
seems to have been written simply to confute his
friend Matthew Arnold's dictum about poetry being
a criticism of life! "Dipsychus" is crammed with
"criticism of life"; but this does not bring it into
line, *qua* poetry, with Keats' "Eve of St. Mark,"
which is almost devoid of such criticism.

That special bitterness of spirit, to be found
in "Dipsychus," was again provoked by the in-
compatibility of his life at University Hall, which
had for him many of the spiritual disadvantages of
orthodox Oxford, with few of its compensations.
"This was without doubt," says Mrs. Clough, "the
dreariest, loneliest period of his life, and he became
compressed and reserved to a degree quite unusual

with him, both before and afterwards. He shut himself up, and went through his life in silence."

One of the few events that helped to save the situation was the friendship he formed at this time with Carlyle, and his earlier acquaintance with Emerson clearly helped him to his next step, which came after two years of University Hall. He decided to leave England and go to Cambridge, Massachusetts; where he arrived in October 1852. The brighter air, the more alert life, of America proved stimulating; but just as he was beginning to define his circle there, and to reconcile himself to the Transatlantic distance from home, he was recalled by the offer of an appointment in the Education Office. He returned home in July 1853. Writing immediately upon his return to his friend, Professor C. Eliot Norton, he said, "I like America best, and but for the greater security which one has in a fixed salary, would give up all thought of staying here at once." However, he was not to see America again.

Probably the work and the confinement of the Council Office, from which many of his letters were dated henceforth, were too much for an

already shaken constitution. His marriage, and
the happiness it brought him, could not restore his
youth. Five or six years of this London life, and
his health began visibly to fail. In 1860 he re-
ceived a long leave of absence, and stayed at
Malvern, and later went to Freshwater, in the Isle
of Wight. Next April he went to the South of
Europe ; visited Greece, saw Constantinople, and
wrote the first of the " Mari Magno" poems, feeling
a revival in him of his old feeling for poetry. In
June he was in England for a few weeks ; then
was ordered south again, and went to Auvergne
and the Pyrenees, where he continued the " Mari
Magno" tales. In August he met the Tennysons,
then lodging at Luchon ; and again at Cauterets.
In September his wife met him at Paris, and with
her he retook his travels, passing through Switzer-
land to the Italian Lakes. At Stresa, on Lake
Maggiore, he seems to have acquired the first
slight touch of the malarial fever, which he was too
weak to resist. They travelled on to Florence, and
there he gradually sank, after struggling, and more
than once apparently rallying, so far as to write the
last of his " Mari Magno" poems, which seems to

have filled his thoughts up to the end. Towards the end, the fever left him ; but he was tired out, and paralysis (which was hereditary in his family) ended the story. He died on the 13th of November 1861, in his forty-third year.

"*Fiat voluntas!* Let us go forward to our manifest destiny with content, or at least resignation, and bravely fill up the trench, which our nobler successors may thus be able to pass."

There spoke Clough, the characteristic spirit of the man and the poet, in his "Letters of Parepidemus," which, with his other letters and prose remains, afford an indispensable interpretation of his poetry. Clough's interest as an original mind, seeking for a more modern adjustment of the old and new poetics, or the old and new ethics, than Oxford provided or sanctioned, needs indeed that one should read all he wrote. He had not time to finish his performance, but it leaves one as it is with a profound sense of his potentiality, by ending on the finer music of his "Mari Magno," whose last line breaks off significantly with the words :

"I and my friend have seen our friends no more."

E. R.

The Bothie.

1.

Socii Cratera Coronant.

THE BOTHIE.

I.

IT was the afternoon; and the sports were all but
over.
Long had the stone been put, tree cast, and thrown the
hammer;
Up the perpendicular hill, Sir Hector so called it,
Eight stout shepherds and gillies had run, two wondrous
quickly;
Run too the course on the level had been; the leaping
was over:
Last in the show of dress, a novelty recently added,
Noble ladies their prizes adjudged for costume that was
perfect,
Turning the clansmen about, who stood with upraised
elbows;
Bowing their eye-glassed brows, and fingering kilt and
sporran.
It was four of the clock, and the sports were all but over,
Therefore the Oxford party went off to adorn for the
dinner.

Be it recorded in song who was first, who last, in
    dressing.
Hope was the first, black-tied, white-waistcoated, simple,
    His Honour ;
For the postman made out he was son to the Earl of Ilay,
(As indeed he was, to the younger brother, the Colonel),
Treated him therefore with special respect ; doffed
    bonnet, and ever
Called him his Honour : his Honour he therefore was at
    the cottage,
Always his Honour at least ; sometimes the Viscount of
    Ilay.

Hope was first, his Honour, and next to his Honour
    the Tutor.
Still more plain the Tutor, the grave man, nicknamed
    Adam,
White-tied, clerical, silent, with antique square-cut
    waistcoat
Formal, unchanged, of black cloth, but with sense and
    feeling beneath it ;
Skilful in Ethics and Logic, in Pindar and Poets un-
    rivalled ;
Shady in Latin, said Lindsay, but *topping* in Plays and
    Aldrich.

Somewhat more splendid in dress, in a waistcoat work
    of a lady,
Lindsay succeeded ; the lively, the cheery, cigar-loving
    Lindsay,

Lindsay the ready of speech, the Piper, the Dialectician,
This was his title from Adam because of the words he
　invented,
Who in three weeks had created a dialect new for the
　party,
Master in all that was new, of whate'er was recherché
　and racy.
Master of newest inventions, and ready deviser of newer;
This was his title from Adam, but mostly they called him
　the Piper.
Lindsay succeeded, the lively, the cheery, cigar-loving
　Lindsay.

Hewson and Hobbes were down at the matutine bath-
　ing; of course too
Arthur Audley, the bather par excellence, Glory of
　Headers,
Arthur they called him for love and for euphony; so
　were they bathing,
There where in mornings was custom, where over a
　ledge of granite
Into a granite basin descended the amber torrent.
There were they bathing and dressing; it was but a step
　from the cottage,
Only the road and larches and ruinous millstead between.
Hewson and Hobbes followed quick upon Adam; on
　them followed Arthur.

Airlie descended the last, splendescent as god of
　Olympus;

Blue, half-doubtfully blue, was the coat that had white
    silk facings,
Waistcoat blue, coral-buttoned, the white tie finely ad-
    justed,
Coral moreover the studs on a shirt as of crochet of
    women :
When for ten minutes already the four-wheel had stood
    at the gateway,
He, like a god, came leaving his ample Olympian chamber.
And in the four-wheel they drove to the place of the
    clansmen's meeting.

So in the four-wheel they came; and Donald the
    innkeeper showed them
Up to the barn where the dinner should be. Four tables
    were in it ;
Two at the top and the bottom, a little upraised from the
    level,
These for Chairman and Croupier, and gentry fit to be
    with them,
Two lengthways in the midst for keeper and gillie and
    peasant.
Here were clansmen many in kilt and bonnet assembled;
Keepers a dozen at least ; the Marquis's targeted gillies ;
Pipers five or six, among them the young one, the
    drunkard ;
Many with silver brooches, and some with those brilliant
    crystals
Found amid granite-dust on the frosty scalp of the Cairn
    Gorm ;

But with snuff-boxes all, and all their boxes using.
Here too were Catholic Priest, and Established Minister standing,
One to say grace before, the other after the dinner;
Catholic Priest; for many still clung to the Ancient Worship;
And Sir Hector's father himself had built them a chapel;
So stood Priest and Minister, near to each other, but silent,
One to say grace before, the other after the dinner.
Hither anon too came the shrewd, ever-ciphering Factor,
Hither anon the Attaché, the Guardsman mute and stately,
Hither from lodge and bothie in all the adjoining shootings
Members of Parliament many, forgetful of votes and blue-books,
Here, amid heathery hills, upon beast and bird of the forest,
Venting the murderous spleen of the endless Railway Committee.
Hither the Marquis of Ayr, and Dalgarnish Earl and Croupier,
And at their side, amid murmurs of welcome, long-looked for, himself too,
Eager, the grey but boy-hearted Sir Hector, the Chief and the Chairman.

Then was the dinner served, and the minister asked a blessing,

And to the viands before them with knife and with fork
 they beset them ;
Venison, the red and the roe, with mutton ; and grouse
 succeeding ;
Such was the feast, with whisky of course, and at top
 and bottom
Small decanters of sherry, not overchoice, for the gentry.
So to the viands before them with laughter and chat
 they beset them.
And when on flesh and on fowl had appetite duly been
 sated,
Up rose the Catholic Priest and returned God thanks for
 the dinner.
Then on all tables were set black bottles of well-mixed
 toddy.
And, with the bottles and glasses before them, they sat
 digesting,
Talking, enjoying, but chiefly awaiting the toasts and
 speeches.

 Spare me, O mighty Remembrance ! for words to the
 task were unequal,
Spare me, O Mistress of Song ! nor bid me recount
 minutely
All that was said and done o'er the well-mixed tempting
 toddy.
Bid me not show in detail, grimace and gesture painting,
How were healths proposed and drunk with all the
 honours,

Glasses and bonnets waving, and three-times-three thrice
over,
Queen, and Prince, and army, and landlords all, and
keepers ;
Bid me not, grammar defying, repeat from grammar-
defiers
Long constructions strange and plusquam-Thucydidëan,
Tell, how as sudden torrent in time of speat in the
mountain
Hurries six ways at once, and takes at last to the roughest,
Or as the practised rider at Astley's or Franconi's
Skilfully, boldly bestrides many steeds at once in the
gallop,
Crossing from this to that, with one leg here, one yonder,
So, less skilful, but equally bold, and wild as the
torrent,
All through sentences six at a time, unsuspecting of
syntax,
Hurried the lively good-will and garrulous tale of Sir
Hector.
Left to oblivion be it, the memory, faithful as ever,
How the noble Croupier would wind up his word with a
whistle,
How the Marquis of Ayr, with quaint gesticulation,
Floundering on through game and mess-room recollec-
tions,
Gossip of neighbouring forest, praise of targeted gillies,
Anticipation of royal visit, skits at pedestrians,
Swore he would never abandon his country, nor give up
deer-stalking ;

How, too, more brief, and plainer, in spite of Gaelic
 accent,
Highland peasants gave courteous answer to flattering
 nobles.

Two orations alone the memorial song will render ;
For at the banquet's close spake thus the lively Sir Hector,
Somewhat husky with praises exuberant, often repeated,
Pleasant to him and to them, of the gallant Highland
 soldiers
Whom he erst led in the fight ;—somewhat husky, but
 cheery, tho' weary,
Up to them rose and spoke the grey but gladsome chief-
 tain :—

Fill up your glasses once more, my friends—with all
 the honours,
There was a toast which I forgot, which our gallant
 Highland homes have
Always welcomed the stranger, I may say, delighted to see
Fine young men at my table—My friends ! are you ready ?
 the Strangers.
Gentlemen, I drink your healths,—and I wish you—
 with all the honours !

So he said, and the cheers ensued, and all the honours,
All our Collegians were bowed to, the Attaché detecting
 His Honour,
The Guardsman moving to Arthur, the Marquis sidling
 to Airlie,

While the little drunken Piper came across to shake hands
with Lindsay.—

But, while the healths were being drunk, was much
tribulation and trouble,
Nodding and beckoning across, observed of Attaché and
Guardsman:
Adam wouldn't speak,—indeed it was known he couldn't;
Hewson could; and would if they wished; Philip
Hewson the poet,
Hewson the radical hot, hating lords and scorning ladies,
Silent mostly, but often reviling in fire and fury
Feudal tenures, mercantile lords, competition and bishops,
Liveries, armorial bearings, amongst other things the
Game-laws:
He could speak, and was asked to by Adam, but Lindsay
aloud cried,
(Whisky was hot in his brain), Confound it, no, not
Hewson,
An't he cocksure to bring in his eternal political hum-
bug?
However, so it must be, and after due pause of silence,
Waving his hand to Lindsay, and smiling queerly to
Adam,
Up to them rose and spoke the poet and radical Hewson.

I am, I think, perhaps the most perfect stranger present.
I have not, as two or three of my friends, in my veins
some tincture,
Some few ounces of Scottish blood; no, nothing like it.

I am therefore perhaps the fittest to answer and thank
  you.
So I thank you, sir, for myself and for my companions,
Heartily thank you all for this unexpected greeting,
All the more welcome as showing you do not count us
  intruders,
Are not unwilling to see the north and south forgather.
And, surely, seldom have Scotch and English more
  joyously mingled ;
Scarcely with warmer hearts, clearer sense of mutual
  manhood,
Even in tourney, and foray, and fray, and regular battle,
Where the life and the strength come out in the tug and
  tussle,
Scarcely, where man confronted man, and soul clasped
  soul,
Close as the bodies and intertwining limbs of athletic
  wrestlers,
When for a final bout are a day's two champions mated,—
In the grand old times of bows, and bills, and claymorcs,
At the old Flodden-field—Bannockburn—Culloden.
—(And he paused a moment, for breath, and because of
  cheering)—
We are the better friends, I fancy, for that old fighting.
Better friends, inasmuch as we know each other better,
We can now shake hands without subterfuge or shuffling.

  On this passage followed a great tornado of cheering,
Tables were rapped, feet stamped, a glass or two got
  broken :

He, ere the cheers had died wholly away, and while still
    there was stamping,
Added, with a smile, in an altered voice, his sarcastic
    conclusion,

Yet I myself have little claim to this honour of having my
    health drunk.
For I am not a game-keeper, I think, nor a game-
    preserver.

So he said, and sat down, but his satire was not taken.
Only the " men," who were all on their legs as concerned
    in the thanking,
Were a trifle confused, but mostly stared without laughing;
Lindsay alone close facing the chair, shook his fist at the
    speaker.
Only a Liberal member, away at the end of the table,
Started, remembering sadly the chance of a coming elec-
    tion,
Only the Attaché sneered to the Guardsman, who twirled
    his moustachio.
Only the Marquis faced round, but not quite clear of the
    meaning,
Joined with the joyous Sir Hector, who lustily beat on
    the table.
    And soon after the chairman arose, and the feast was
    over :
Now should the barn be cleared and forthwith adorned
    for the dancing,
And our friends, retiring to wait for this consummation,

Were, as they stood in the doorway uncertain, debating
    together,
By the good chieftain so joyous invited hard by to the
    castle.
But as the doorway they quitted, a thin man, clad as the
    Saxon,
Trouser and cap and jacket of home-spun blue, hand-
    woven,
Singled out and said, with determined accent, to Hewson,
Resting his hand on his shoulder, while each in the eyes
    dilating
Firmly scanned each : "Young man, if ye pass through
    the Braes o' Lochaber,
See by the lochside ye come to the Bothie of Toper-na-
    fuosich."

II.

*Et certamen erat, Corydon cum Thyrside,
magnum.*

II.

MORN in yellow and white came broadening out from
    the mountains,
Long ere music and reel were hushed in the barn of the
    dancers.
Duly in matutine bathed before eight some two of the
    party,
There where in mornings was custom, where, over a
    ledge of granite
Into a granite basin descended the amber torrent.
Duly there two plunges each took Philip and Arthur,
Duly in matutine bathed, and read, and wished for
    breakfast ;
Breakfast, commencing at nine, lingered lazily on to
    noon-day.

Tea and coffee were there ; a jug of water for Hewson;
Tea and coffee ; and four cold grouse upon the sideboard;
Cranberry-jam was reserved for tea, and for festive
    occasions :
Gaily they talked as they sat, some late and lazy at
    breakfast,

Some professing a book, some smoking outside at the
  window.
'Neath an aurora soft-pouring a still sheeny tide to the
  zenith,
Hewson and Arthur, with Adam, had walked and got
  home by eleven ;
Hope and the others had stayed till the round sun lighted
  them bedward.
They of the lovely aurora, but these of the lovelier women
Spoke—of noble ladies and rustic girls, their partners.

  Turned to them Hewson, the chartist, the poet, the
    eloquent speaker.
Sick of the very names of your Lady Augustas and Floras
Am I, as ever I was of the dreary botanical titles
Of the exotic plants, their antitypes, in the hothouse :
Roses, violets, lilies for me ! the out-of-door beauties ;
Meadow and woodland sweets, forget-me-nots and hearts-
  ease !
  Pausing awhile, he proceeded anon, for none made
    answer :
Oh, if our high-born girls knew only the grace, the
  attraction,
Labour, and labour alone, can add to the beauty of
  women,
Truly the milliner's trade would quickly, I think, be at
  discount,
All the waste and loss in silk and satin be saved us,
Saved for purposes truly and widely productive——
                                    That's right,

Take off your coat to it, Philip, cried Lindsay outside in
    the garden,
Lindsay, cigar-loving hero, the Piper, the Dialectician,
Take off your coat to it, Philip.
                    Well, well, said Hewson, resuming,
Laugh if you please at my novel economy; listen to this,
    though.
As for myself, and apart from economy wholly, believe
    me,
Never I properly felt the relation of man to woman,
Though to the dancing-master I went, perforce, for a
    quarter,
Where in dismal quadrille, were good-looking girls in
    plenty,
Though, too, school-girl cousins were mine—a bevy of
    beauties,   .
Never (of course you will laugh, but of course all the
    same I shall say it),
Never, believe me, revealed itself to me the sexual
    glory,
Till in some village fields in holidays now getting stupid,
One day sauntering, "long and listless," as Tennyson
    has it,
Long and listless strolling, ungainly in hobbadiboyhood,
Chanced it my eye fell aside on a capless, bonnetless
    maiden,
Bending with three-pronged fork in a garden uprooting
    potatoes.
Was it the air? who can say? or herself, or the charm of
    the labour?

But a new thing was in me; and longing delicious
    possessed me,
Longing to take her and lift her, and put her away from
    her slaving.
Was it to clasp her in lifting, or was it to lift her by
    clasping,
Was it embracing or aiding was most in my mind? hard
    question !
But a new thing was in me, I too was a youth among
    maidens ;
Was it the air, who can say? but in part 'twas the charm
    of the labour.
I was too awkward, too shy, a great deal, be assured, for
    advances ;
Shyly I shambled away, stopping oft, but afraid of
    returning,
Shambled obliquely away, with furtive occasional side-
    look,
Long, though listless no more, in my awkward hobbadi-
    boyhood.
Still, though a new thing was in me, though vernal
    emotion, the secret,   .
Yes, amid prurient talk, the unimparted mysterious
    secret,
Long the growing distress, and celled-up dishonour of
    boyhood,
Recognised now, took its place, a relation, oh bliss !
    unto others ;
Though now the poets, whom love is the key to, revealed
    themselves to me.

And in my dreams by Miranda, her Ferdinand, sat I
  unwearied,
Though all the fuss about girls, the giggling, and toying,
  and coying,
Were not so strange as they had been, so incompre-
  hensible purely;
Still, as before (and as now), balls, dances, and evening
  parties,
Shooting with bows, going shopping together, and hear-
  ing them singing,
Dangling beside them, and turning the leaves on the
  dreary piano,
Offering unneeded arms, performing dull farces of escort,
Seemed like a sort of unnatural up-in-the-air balloon
  work
(Or what to me is as hateful, a riding about in a carriage),
Utter divorcement from work, mother earth, and objects
  of living,
As were gratuitous trifling in presence of business and
  duty,
As does the turning aside of the tourist to look at a land-
  scape
Seem in the steamer or coach to the merchant in haste
  for the city.
Hungry and fainting for food you ask me to join you in
  snapping—
What but a pink paper comfit, with motto romantic
  inside it?
Wishing to stock me a garden, I'm sent to a table of
  nosegays:

Pretty I see it, and sweet ; but they hardly would grow
    in my borders.
Better a crust of black bread than a mountain of paper
    confections,
Better a daisy in earth than a dahlia cut and gathered,
Better a cowslip with root than a prize carnation with-
    out it.

That I allow, said Adam.

                But he with the bit in his teeth, scarce
Breathed a brief moment, and hurried exultingly on with
    his rider,
Far over hillock, and runnel, and bramble, away in the
    champaign,
Snorting defiance and force, the white foam flecking his
    quarters,
Rein hanging loose to his neck, and head projected
    before him.

  Oh, if they knew and considered, unhappy ones ! oh,
    could they see, could
But for a moment discern how the blood of true gallantry
    kindles,
How the old knightly religion, the chivalry semi-quixotic
Stirs in the veins of a man at seeing some delicate woman
Serving him, toiling—for him, and the world ; some ten-
    derest girl, now
Over-weighted, expectant, of him, is it? who shall,
    if only

Duly her burden be lightened,—not wholly removed from
 her, mind you—
Lightened if but by the love, the devotion man only can
 offer,
Grand on her pedestal rise as urn-bearing statue of
 Hellas ;—
Oh, could they feel at such moments how man's heart, as
 into Eden
Carried anew, seems to see, like the gardener of earth
 uncorrupted,
Eve from the hand of her Maker advancing, an helpmeet
 for him,
Eve from his own flesh taken, a spirit restored to his
 spirit ;
Spirit, but not spirit only, himself whatever himself is,
Unto the mystery's end sole helpmate meet to be with
 him ;—
Oh if they saw it and knew it ! we soon should see them
 abandon
Boudoir, toilet, carriage, drawing-room, and ball-room,
Satin for worsted exchange, gros-de-naples for linsey-
 woolsey,
Sandals of silk for clogs, for health lackadaisical fancies !
So feel women, not dolls; so feel the sap of existence
Circulate up through their roots from the far-away centre
 of all things,
Circulate up from the depths to the bud on the twig that
 is topmost !
Yes, we should see them delighted, delighted ourselves
 in the seeing,

Bending with blue cotton gown skirted up over striped
    linsey-woolsey,
Milking the kine in the field, like Rachel, watering cattle,
Rachel, when at the well the predestined beheld and
    kissed her ;
Or with pail upon head, like Dora, beloved of Alexis,
Comely, with well-poised pail over neck arching soft to
    the shoulders,
Comely in gracefullest act, one arm uplifted to stay it,
Home from the river or pump moving stately and calm
    to the laundry ;
Aye, doing household work, as many sweet girls I have
    looked at,
Needful household work, which some one, after all, must
    do,
Needful, graceful therefore, as washing, cooking, scouring,
Or, if you please, with the fork in the garden, uprooting
    potatoes—

—Or high-kilted, perhaps, cried Lindsay, at last suc-
    cessful,
Lindsay this long time swelling with scorn and pent-up
    fury,
Or high-kilted, perhaps, as once at Dundee I saw them,
Petticoats up to their knees, or, it might be, a little bit
    higher,
Matching their lily-white legs with the clothes that they
    trod in the wash-tub !

Laughter loud ensued ; and seeing the Tutor embarrassed,

It was from them, I suppose, said Arthur, smiling sedately,
Lindsay learnt the tune we all have learnt from Lindsay,
For oh, he was a roguey, the Piper o' Dundee.

Laughter ensued again; and the Tutor still slightly embarrassed
Picked at the fallen thread, and commenced a reply to Hewson.
There's truth in what you say, though truly much distorted;
These, I think, no less than other agaceries cloy one;
Still there's truth, I own, I perfectly understand you.

While the Tutor was gathering his thoughts, continued Arthur,
Is not all this just the same that one hears at common-room breakfasts,
Or perhaps Trinity wines, about Gothic buildings and beauty?

And with a start from the sofa came Hobbes; with a cry from the sofa,
There where he lay, the great Hobbes, contemplative, corpulent, witty,
Author forgotten and silent of currentest phrase and fancy,
Mute and exuberant by turns, a fountain at intervals playing,
Mute and abstracted, or strong and abundant as rain in the tropics;

Studious; careless of dress; inobservant; by smooth
    persuasions
Lately decoyed into kilt on example of Hope and the
    Piper,
Hope an Antinous mere, Hyperion of calves the Piper.

    Beautiful! cried he, upleaping, analogy perfect to
    madness!
O inexhaustible source of thought, shall I call it, or fancy!
Wonderful spring, at whose touch doors fly, what a vista
    disclosing!   .
Exquisite germ! Ah no, crude fingers shall not soil
    thee;
Rest, lovely pearl, in my brain, and slowly mature in the
    oyster.

    While at the exquisite pearl they were laughing and
    corpulent oyster,
Ah, could they only be taught, he resumed, by a Pugin
    of women,
How even churning and washing, the dairy, the scullery
    duties,
Wait but a touch to redeem and convert them to charms
    and attractions,
Scrubbing requires for true grace but frank and artistical
    handling,
And the removal of slops to be ornamentally treated.

    Philip, who speaks like a book,—retiring and pausing,
    he added,

Philip here, who speaks—like a folio, say'st thou, Piper?
Philip shall write us a book, a Treatise upon *The Laws of
Architectural Beauty in Application to Women;*
Illustrations, of course, and a Parker's Glossary pendent,
Where shall in specimen seen be the sculliony stumpy-
   columnar
(Which to a reverent taste is perhaps the most moving of
   any)
Rising to grace of true woman in English the Early and
   Later,
Charming us still in fulfilling the Richer and Loftier
   stages,
Lost, ere we end, in the Lady-Debased and the Lady-
   Flamboyant:
Thence why in satire and spite too merciless onward
   pursue her
Hither to hideous close, Modern-Florid, modern-fine-
   lady?
No, I will leave it to you, my Philip, my Pugin of
   women.

   Leave it to Arthur, said Adam, to think of, and not
      to play with.
You are young, you know, he said, resuming, to Philip,
You are young, he proceeded, with something of fervour,
   to Hewson,
You are a boy; when you grow to a man, you'll find
   things alter.
You will learn to seek the good, to scorn the attractive,
Scorn all mere cosmetics, as now of rank and fashion,

Delicate hands, and wealth, so then of poverty also,
Poverty truly attractive, more truly, I bear you witness.
Good, wherever found, you will choose, be it humble or
    stately,
Happy if only you find, and finding do not lose it.
Yes, we must seek what is good, it always and it only;
Not indeed absolute good,—good for us, as is said in the
    Ethics,
That which is good for ourselves, our proper selves, our
    best selves;
This if you find in another, desert not, whatever you call it,
Call it a likeness of souls, call it anything else you fancy,
Perfect response, if you please, to what would in us be
    most perfect,
Answer most searching to what in ourselves is profoundest
    and shyest:
This if you find in another, desert not, wherever you find it,
Happy if only you find, and finding do not lose it!
Ah, you have much to learn, we can't know all at twenty,
You are a boy, as I said; when you grow to a man, you'll
    say so.

   This was the answer he had from the eager impetuous
    Hewson:
Yes, I say it now, I know I'm young; and know, too,
How the grown-up man puts by the youthful instinct,
Learns to deal with the good, but, what good is, discerns
    not;
Learns to handle the helm, but breaks the compass to
    steer by;

In the intuitive loses far more than his gain discursive;
Or, in the lingo you love, the lingo emphatic of Aldrich,
Gets up the form syllogistic, ignoring the premiss and
matter.

While he spoke, Adam rose, sat again, and dropping
his eyelids
Bowed his face in his hands, and rested his hands on the
table;
So for a minute he sat—the one first minute of silence;
Looked up at last, and laughed, and answered, speaking
serenely,
Speaking serenely, but still with a moisture about the
eyelids:

Truly, queer fellow is Hewson! for bidding him choose
good only,
Thus to upbraid me with years, chill years that are
thickening to forty.
Nay, never talk! listen now! What I say you can't
apprehend—
No, you are looking elsewhere. You will not ever, I
fancy—
Till you ignore your premiss, repairing the loss by a new
one,
Till you discard your compass, if not for instruction in
steering,
Yet to purchase a better, and pay, I suppose, for the
purchase.
So much in repartee—but let us return to the question.

Partly you rest on truth, old truth, the duty of Duty,
Partly on error, you long for equality.

      Aye, cried the Piper,
That's the sore place, that confounded Egalité, French
  manufacture;
He is the same as the Chartist who made an address in
  Ireland,
What, and is not one man, fellow-men, as good as another?
Faith, replied Pat, *and a deal better too!*

      So rattled the Piper.

But undisturbed in his tenor, the Tutor:
      Partly in error
Seeking equality, *is not one woman as good as another?*
I with the Irishman answer, *Yes, better too;* the poorer
Better full oft than richer, than loftier better the lower.—
Irrespective of wealth and of poverty, pain and enjoy-
  ment,
Women all have their duties, the one as well as the
  other;
Are all duties alike? Do all alike fulfil them?
It is to these we must look, and in these we are not on a
  level;
Neither in these, nor in gifts, nor attainments, nor
  requirements.
However noble the dream of equality, mark you, Philip,
Nowhere equality reigns in God's sublime creations,
Star is not equal to star, nor blossom the same as
  blossom;

Herb is not equal to herb, any more than planet to
 planet.
True, that the plant should be rooted in earth, I granted
 you wholly,
And that the daisy in earth surpasses the cut carnation,
Only, the rooted carnation surpasses the rooted daisy:
There is one glory of daisies, another of carnations;
Foolish were budding carnation, in gay parterre by
 greenhouse,
Should it decline to accept the nurture the gardener
 gives it,
Should it refuse to expand to sun and genial summer,
Simply because the field-daisy, that grows in the grass-
 plat beside it,
Cannot, for some cause or other, develop and be a car-
 nation.
Would not the daisy itself petition its scrupulous neigh-
 bour?
Up, grow, bloom, and forget me; be beautiful even to
 proudness,
E'en for the sake of myself and other poor daisies like me.
Rooted in earth should it be, carnation alike or daisy,
That I grant, and refer you to Shakespeare on gilly-
 flowers,
Where in the Winter's Tale Leontes Perdita questions.
Education and manners, accomplishments, refinements,
Waltz, peradventure, and polka, the knowledge of music
 and drawing,
All these things are Nature's, to Nature dear and
 precious.

We must all do something, man, woman alike, I own
    it;
Yes, but woman-and-man in lady-and-gentleman is not
Lost, extinct; it lives; if not, God help them, change
    them !
We must all do something, and in my judgment do it
In our station; independent of it, but not regardless;
Holding it, not for enjoyment, but because we cannot
    change it.

Ah! replied Philip, Alas! the noted phrase of the
    prayer-book,
*Doing our duty in that state of life to which God has
    called us,*
Seems to me always to mean, when the little rich boys
    say it,
Standing in velvet frock by mamma's brocaded flounces,
Eyeing her gold-fastened book and the chain and watch
    at her bosom,
Seems to me always to mean *Eat, drink, and never mind
    others.*

  Nay, replied Adam, smiling, so far your economy
    leads me;
Velvet and gold and brocade are nowise to my fancy;
Benefit of trade, I see, is mockery vile and delusion.
Nay, he added, believe me, I like luxurious living
Ever as little as you, and grieve in my soul not seldom,
More for the rich indeed than the poor, who are not so
    guilty.

Ah ! replied Philip again, but as for the rest of the
    story,
Truly I see a good deal in the daisy-carnation fable ;
Though I should like to be clear what standing in the
    earth means.
But, as you said to me when this long discussion started,
There's truth in what you say, though I *don't* quite
    understand you.

So the discussion ended : and Arthur rose up smiling,
Now, quoth he, that Philip daren't bully you more, it is
    my turn.
How will my argument please you ?   To-morrow we
    start on our travel.

And took up Hope the chorus :
                            To-morrow we start on our
    travel,
Lo, the weather is golden, the weather-glass, say they,
    rising ;
Four weeks here have we read ; four weeks will we read
    hereafter ;
Three weeks hence will return, and revisit our dismal
    classics,
Three weeks hence readjust our visions of classes and
    classics.
Fare ye well, meantime, forgotten, unnamed, undreamt
    of,
History, science, and poets ! lo, deep in dustiest cup-
    board,

Thookydid, Olorus' son, Halimoosian, here lieth buried !
Slumber in Liddell-and-Scott, O musical chaff of old
    Athens,
Dishes, and fishes, bird, beast, and sesquipedalian black-
    guard !
Sleep, weary ghosts, be at peace, and abide in your
    lexicon-limbo !
Sleep, as in lava for ages your Herculanean kindred,
Sleep, and for aught that I care, 'the sleep that knows
    no waking,'
Æschylus, Sophocles, Homer, Herodotus, Pindar, and
    Plato,
Three weeks hence be it time to exhume our dreary
    classics.

    And in the chorus joined Lindsay, the Piper, the Dia-
    lectician.
Three weeks hence we return to the *shop* and the *wash-*
    hand-stand-basin,
Three weeks hence unbury *Thicksides* and *hairy* Aldrich.

    But the Tutor enquired, the grave man, nicknamed
    Adam,
'Who are they that go, and when do they promise
    returning?'
And a silence ensued, and the Tutor himself continued,
'Airlie remains, I presume,' he continued, 'and Hobbes
    and Hewson;
Lindsay and Arthur and Hope to verify Black are a
    quorum.'

Answer was made him by Philip, the poet, the
    eloquent speaker,
'Airlie remains, I presume,' was the answer, 'and
    Hobbes, peradventure';
Tarry let Airlie Mayfairly, and Hobbes, brief-kilted
    hero,
Tarry let Hobbes in kilt, and Airlie 'abide in his
    breeches';
Tarry let these, and read,—four Pindars apiece, an' it
    like them!
Weary of reading am I, and weary of walks prescribed us;
Weary of Ethic and Logic, of Rhetoric yet more weary,
Eager to range over heather unfettered of gillie and
    marquis,
I will away with the rest, and bury my *hairy* 'Tottle.

And, to the Tutor, rejoining Be mindful; you go up at
    Easter,
This was the answer returned by Philip, the Pugin of
    women.
Good are the Ethics, I wis; Good Absolute; not for me,
    though;
Good, too, Logic, of course; in itself; but not in fine
    weather.
Three weeks hence, with the rain, to Prudence, Temper-
    ance, Justice,
Virtues Moral and Mental, with Latin prose included,
Three weeks hence we return, to cares of classes and
    classics,
I will away with the rest, and bury my *hairy* 'Tottle.

But the Tutor inquired, the grave man, nicknamed
  Adam,
Where do you mean to go, and whom do you mean to
  visit ?

And he was answered by Hope, the Viscount, His
  Honour, of Ilay.
Kitcat, a Trinity *coach*, has a party at Drumnadrochet,
Up on the side of Loch Ness, in the beautiful valley of
  Urquhart ;
Mainwaring says they will lodge us, and feed us, and
  give us a lift too ;
Only they talk ere long to remove to Glenmorison.
  Then at
Castleton, high in Braemar, strange home, with his
  earliest party,
Harrison, fresh from the Schools, has James, and Jones,
  and Lauder.
Thirdly, a Cambridge man I know, Smith, a senior
  wrangler,
With a mathematical score hangs out at Inverary.

Finally, too, from the kilt and the sofa, said Hobbes in
  conclusion,
Finally, Philip must hunt for that home of the probable
  poacher,
Hid in the braes of Lochaber, the Bothie of What-did-
  he-call-it.
Hopeless of you and of us, of gillies and marquises
  hopeless,

Weary of Ethic and Logic, of Rhetoric yet more weary,
There shall he, smit by the charm of a lovely potato-
    uprooter,
Study the question of sex in the Bothie of What-did-he-
    call-it.

III.

Namque canebat uti—

III.

So in the golden morning they parted and went to the
westward.

And in the cottage with Airlie and Hobbes remained the
Tutor ;

Reading nine hours a day with the Tutor Hobbes and
Airlie ;

One between bathing and breakfast, and six before it was
dinner,

(Breakfast at eight, at four, after bathing again, the
dinner),

Finally, two after walking and tea, from nine to eleven.

Airlie and Adam at evening their quiet stroll together

Took on the terrace-road, with the western hills before
them ;

Hobbes, only rarely a third, now and then in the cottage
remaining,

E'en after dinner eupeptic, would rush yet again to his
reading ;

Other times, stung by the œstrum of some swift-working
conception,

Ranged, tearing on in his fury, an Io-cow, through the
mountains,

Heedless of scenery, heedless of bogs, and of perspiration,
Far on the peaks, unwitting, the hares and ptarmigan
  starting.

And the three weeks past, the three weeks, three days
  over,
Neither letter had come, nor casual tidings any,
And the pupils grumbled, the Tutor became uneasy,
And in the golden weather they wondered, and watched
  to the westward.

There is a stream—I name not its name, lest
  inquisitive tourist
Hunt it, and make it a lion, and get it at last into guide-
  books—
Springing far off from a loch unexplored in the folds of
  great mountains,
Falling two miles through rowan and stunted alder,
  enveloped
Then for four more in a forest of pine, where broad and
  ample
Spreads to convey it the glen with heathery slopes on
  both sides:
Broad and fair the stream, with occasional falls and
  narrows;
But, where the lateral glen approaches the vale of the
  river,
Met and blocked by a huge interposing mass of granite,
Scarce by a channel deep-cut, raging up, and raging
  onward,

Forces its flood through a passage, so narrow, a lady
    would step it.
There, across the great rocky wharves, a wooden bridge
    goes,
Carrying a path to the forest; below, three hundred
    yards, say,
Lower in level some twenty-five feet, through flats of
    shingle,
Stepping-stones and a cart-track cross in the open valley.

But in the interval here the boiling, pent-up water
Frees itself by a final descent, attaining a basin,
Ten feet wide and eighteen long, with whiteness and
    fury
Occupied partly, but mostly pellucid, pure, a mirror;
Beautiful there for the colour derived from green rocks
    under;
Beautiful, most of all, where beads of foam uprising
Mingle their clouds of white with the delicate hue of the
    stillness.
Cliff over cliff for its sides, with rowan and pendent
    birch-boughs,
Here it lies, unthought of above at the bridge and
    pathway,
Still more concealed from below by wood and rocky
    projection,
You are shut in, left alone with yourself and perfection
    of water,
Hid on all sides, left alone with yourself and the goddess
    of bathing.

Here, the pride of the plunger, you stride the fall and
clear it ;
Here, the delight of the bather, you roll in beaded
sparklings,
Here into pure green depth drop down from lofty ledges.

Hither a month agone, they had come, and discovered ;
hither
(Long a design, but long unaccountably left unaccom-
plished),
Leaving the well-known bridge and pathway above to the
forest,
Turning below from the track of the carts over stone and
shingle,
Piercing a wood, and skirting a narrow and natural
causeway
Under the rocky wall that hedges the bed of the streamlet,
Rounded a craggy point, and saw on a sudden before
them,
Slabs of rock, and a tiny beach, and perfection of water,
Picture-like beauty, seclusion sublime, and the goddess
of bathing.
There they bathed, of course, and Arthur, the Glory of
Headers,
Leapt from the ledges with Hope, he twenty feet, he
thirty :
There, overbold, great Hobbes from a ten-foot height
descended,
Prone, as a quadruped, prone, with hands and feet
protending :

There in the sparkling champagne, ecstatic, they shrieked
and shouted.

"Hobbes's gutter" the Piper entitles the spot, profanely,
Hope "the Glory" would have, after Arthur, the glory
of headers :
But,—for before they departed, in shy and fugitive reflex,
Here in the eddies and there did the splendour of Jupiter
glimmer,—
Adam adjudged it the name of Hesperus, star of the
evening.

Hither, to Hesperus, now, the star of evening above
them,
Come in their lonelier walk the pupils twain and
Tutor :
Turned from the track of the carts, and passing the stone
and shingle,
Piercing the wood, and skirting the stream by the natural
causeway,
Rounded the craggy point, and now at their ease looked
up; and
Lo, on the beach, expecting the plunge, not cigarless, the
Piper.—

And they looked, and wondered, incredulous, looking
yet once more.
Yes, it was he, on the ledge, bare-limbed, an Apollo,
down-gazing,

Eyeing one moment the beauty, the life, ere he flung
    himself in it,
Eyeing through eddying green waters the green-tinting
    floor underneath them,
Eyeing the bead on the surface, the bead, like a cloud
    rising to it,
Drinking in, deep in his soul, the beautiful hue and the
    clearness,
Arthur, the shapely, the brave, the unboasting, the Glory
    of Headers;
Yes, and with fragrant weed by his knapsack, spectator
    and critic,
Seated on slab by the margin, the Piper, the Cloud-
    compeller.

    Yes, they were come; were restored to the party, its
    grace and its gladness,
Yes, were here, as of old; the light-giving orb of the
    household,
Arthur, the shapely, the tranquil, the strength-and-con-
    tentment-diffusing,
In the pure presence of whom none could quarrel long,
    nor be pettish,
And the gay fountain of mirth, their own dear genial Piper.
Yes, they were come, were here: but Hewson and Hope,
    where they, then?
Are they behind, travel-sore, or ahead, going straight by
    the pathway?

    And from his seat and cigar spoke the Piper, the Cloud-
    compeller.

Hope with the uncle abideth for shooting. Ah me,
    were I with him !
Ah, good boy that I am, to have stuck to my word and
    my reading !
Good, good boy to be here, far away, who might be at
    Balloch,
Only one day to have stayed who might have been
    welcome for seven,
Seven whole days in castle and forest—gay in the mazy
Moving, imbibing the rosy, and pointing a gun at the
    horny !

    And the Tutor impatient, expectant, interrupted,
Hope with the uncle, and Hewson—with him? or where
    have you left him?

    And from his seat and cigar spoke the Piper, the
    Cloud-compeller :
Hope with the uncle and Hewson—why, Hewson we
    left in Rannoch,
By the loch-side and the pines, in a farmer's house,—
    reflecting,—
Helping to shear and dry clothes, and it may be, uproot
    potatoes,
Studying the question of sex, though not at What-did-he-
    call-it?

    And the Tutor's countenance fell, perplexed, dumb-
    founded
Stood he—slow and with pain disengaging jest from
    earnest.

He is not far from home, said Arthur from the water,
He will be with us to-morrow, at latest, or the next day.

And he was even more reassured by the Piper's
rejoinder :
Can he have come by the mail, and have got to the
cottage before us?

So to the cottage they went, and Philip was not at the
cottage ;
But by the mail was a letter from Hope, who himself was
to follow.

Two whole days and nights succeeding brought not
Philip,
Two whole days and nights exhausted not question and
story.

For it was told, the Piper narrating, corrected of
Arthur,
Often by word corrected, more often by smile and motion,
How they had been to Iona, to Staffa, to Skye, to
Culloden,
Seen Loch Awe, Loch Tay, Loch Fyne, Loch Ness,
Loch Arkaig,
Been up Ben-nevis, Ben-more, Ben-cruachan, Ben-muick-
dhui ;
How they had walked, and eaten, and drunken, and
slept in kitchens,
Slept upon floors of kitchens, and tasted the real Glen-
livat,

Walked up perpendicular hills, and also down them,
Hither and thither had been, and this and that had
witnessed,
Left not a thing to be done, and had not a *brown*
remaining.
For it was told withal, he telling, and he correcting,
How they had met, they believed, with St. John, the
muckle-hart-slayer,
How in the race they had run, and beaten the gillies of
Rannoch,
How in forbidden glens, in Mar and midmost Athol,
Philip insisting hotly, and Arthur and Hope compliant,
They had defied the keepers ; the Piper alone protesting,
Liking the fun, it was plain, in his heart, but tender of
game-law ;
Yea, too, in Meäly glen, the heart of Lochiel's fair forest,
Where Scotch firs are darkest and amplest, and intermingle
Grandly with rowan and ash—in Mar you have no
ashes,
There the pine is alone, or relieved by the birch and the
alder—
How in Meäly fair, while stags were starting before, they
Made the watcher believe they were guests from
Achnacarry.

And there was told moreover, he telling, the other
correcting,
Often by word, more often by mute significant motion,
Much of the Cambridge coach and his pupils at Inverary,
Huge barbarian pupils, expanded in infinite series,

4

Firing off signal guns (great scandal) from window to
 window
(For they were lodging perforce in distant and numerous
 houses),
Signals when, one retiring, another should go to the
 Tutor :—
Much, too, of Kitcat, of course, and the party at
 Drumnadrochet,
Mainwaring, Foley and Fraser, their idleness horrid and
 dog-cart ;
Drumnadrochet was *seedy*, Glenmorison *adequate*, but at
Castleton high in Braemar were the *clippingest* places
 for bathing ;
One by the bridge in the village, indecent, *the Town Hall*
 christened,
Where howbeit had Lauder been bathing, and Harrison
 also,
Harrison even, the Tutor; another like Hesperus here, and
Up to the Water of Eye half-a-dozen at least, all *stunners*.

And it was told, the Piper narrating and Arthur
 correcting ;
Colouring he, dilating, magniloquent, glorying in picture,
He to a matter-of-fact still softening, paring, abating :
He to the great might-have-been uproaring, sublime and
 ideal,
He to the merest it-was restricting, diminishing, dwarfing,
River to streamlet reducing, and fall to slope subduing;

So it was told, the Piper narrating, corrected of Arthur,

How under Linn of Dee, where over rocks, between rocks,
Freed from prison the river comes, pouring, rolling, rushing,
Then at a sudden descent goes sliding, gliding, unbroken,
Falling, sliding, gliding, in narrow space collected,
Save for a curl at the end where the curve rejoins the
    level,
Save for a ripple at last, a sheeted descent unbroken,—
How to the elements offering their bodies, downshooting
    the fall, they
Mingled themselves with the flood and the force of
    imperious water.

And it was told, too, Arthur narrating, the Piper
    correcting,
How, as one comes to the level, the weight of the down-
    ward impulse
Carries the head under water, delicious, ineffable ; how the
Piper, here ducked and blinded, got astray, and borne
    off by the current,
Wounded his lily-white thighs, below, at the craggy
    corner.

And it was told, the Piper resuming, corrected of
    Arthur,
More by word than motion, change ominous, noted of
    Adam,
How at the floating bridge of Laggan, one morning at
    sunrise,
Came in default of the ferryman, out of her bed a brave
    lassie ;

And as Philip and she together were turning the handles,
By which the chain is wound that works it across the
water,
Hands intermingled with hands, and at last, as they
stepped from the boatie,
Turning about, they saw lips also mingle with lips ; but
That was flatly denied and loudly exclaimed at by Arthur :
How at the General's hut, the inn by the Fall of Foyers,
Where o'er the loch looks at you the summit of
Méalfourvónie,
How here, too, he was hunted at morning, and found in
the kitchen,
Watching the porridge being made, pronouncing them
smoked for certain,
Watching the porridge being made, and asking the lassie
that made them
What was the Gaelic for girl, and what was the Gaelic
for pretty;
How in confusion he shouldered his knapsack, yet
blushingly stammered,
Waving a hand to the lassie, that blushingly bent o'er
the porridge,
Something outlandish—Slan-something, Slanleat, he
believed, Caleg Looach,
That was the Gaelic, it seemed, for ' I bid you good-bye,
bonnie lassie ; '
Arthur allowed it was true, not of Philip, but of the Piper.

And it was told by the Piper, while Arthur looked out
at the window,

How in thunder and in rain—it is wetter far to the
westward—
Thunder and rain and wind, losing heart and road, they
were welcomed,
Welcomed, and three days detained, at a farm by the
lochside of Rannoch ;
How in the three days' detention was Philip observed to
be smitten,
Smitten by golden-haired Katie, the youngest and
comeliest daughter ;
Was he not seen, even Arthur observed it, from breakfast
to bedtime,
Following her motions with eyes ever brightening,
softening ever ?
Did he not fume, fret, and fidget to find her stand waiting
at table ?
Was he not one mere St. Vitus' dance, when he saw her
at nightfall
Go through the rain to fetch peat, through beating rain
to the peat-stack ?
How it so happened a dance was given by Grant of
Glenurchie,
And with the farmer they went, as the farmer's guests,
to attend it ;
Philip stayed dancing till daylight—and evermore with
Katie ;
How the whole next afternoon he was with her away in
the shearing ;
And the next morning ensuing was found in the ingle
beside her

Kneeling, picking the peats from her apron,—blowing
together,
Both, between laughing, with lips distended, to kindle
the embers;
Lips were so near to lips, one living cheek to another,
Though, it was true, he was shy, strangely shy,—yet it
was not nature,
Was not nature, the Piper averred, there shouldn't be
kissing.
Then when they packed up their knapsack at noon, and
proposed to be starting,
Philip professed he was lame, would leave in the morning
and follow;
Follow he did not; do burns, when you go up a glen,
follow after?
Follow he had not; nor left; do needles leave the
loadstone?
Nay too, they turned after starting, and looked through
the trees at the corner,
Lo, on the rocks by the lake there he was, the lassie
beside him,
Lo, there he was, stooping by her, and helping with
stones from the water
Safe in the wind to keep down the clothes she would
spread for the drying.
There they had left him, and there, if Katie was there,
was Philip,
There drying clothes, making fires, making love, getting
on too by this time,
Though he was shy, so exceedingly shy.

You may say so, said Arthur,
For the first time they had known with a peevish
    intonation,—
Did not the Piper himself flirt more in a single evening,
Namely, with Janet the elder, than Philip in all our
    sojourn?
Philip had stayed, it was true; the Piper was loth to
    depart, too,
Harder his parting from Janet than e'en from the
    keeper at Balloch;
And it was certain that Philip was lame—

                    Yes, in his excuses!
Answered the Piper, indeed!—

              Nay, truly, said Hobbes interposing,
Did you not say she was seen every day in her beauty
    and bedgown
Doing plain household work, as washing, cooking,
    scouring!
How could he help but love her? nor lacked there of
    course the attraction
That, in a blue cotton print tucked up over striped linsey-
    woolsey,
Barefoot, barelegged, he beheld her, with arms bare up
    to the elbows,
Bending with fork in her hand in a garden uprooting
    potatoes?
Is not Katie as Rachel, and is not Philip a Jacob?
Truly Jacob, supplanting a hairy Highland Esau!

Shall he not, love-entertained, feed sheep for the Laban
    of Rannoch?
O happy patriarch he, the long servitude ended of wooing,
If when he wake in the morning he find not a Leah
    beside him!
    But the Tutor inquired, who had bit his lip to bleeding,
How far off is the place? who will guide me there to-
    morrow?

But by the mail, ere the morrow, came Hope, and
    brought new tidings;
Round by Rannoch had come, and Philip was not at
    Rannoch;
He had left that noon, an hour ago.

                              With the lassie?
With her? the Piper exclaimed: undoubtedly! By great
    Jingo!
And upon that he arose, slapping both his thighs, like a
    hero,
Partly for emphasis only, to mark his conviction, but also
Part in delight at the fun, and the joy of eventful living.

    Really I did not inquire, answered Hope, but I hardly
    think it;
Janet, Piper, your friend, I saw, and she didn't say so,
Though she asked a good deal about Philip, and where
    he was gone to;
One odd thing, by-the-bye, he continued, befell me while
    with her;

Standing beside her, I saw a girl pass; I thought I had
    seen her,
Somewhat remarkable-looking, elsewhere; and asked
    what her name was;
Elspie Mackaye, was the answer, the daughter of David!
    she's stopping
Just above there, with her uncle. And David Mackaye,
    where lives he?
It's away west, she replied; they call it Toper-na-fuosich.

IV.

Ut vidi, ut perii, ut me malus abstulit error.

IV.

So in the golden weather they waited.   But Philip
  came not.
Sunday six days thence a letter arrived in his writing —
But, O Muse, that encompassest Earth like the ambient
  ether,
Swifter than steamer or railway or magical missive
  electric,
Belting like Ariel the sphere with the star-like trail of
  thy travel,
Thou, with thy Poet, to mortals mere Post Office second-
  hand knowledge
Leaving, wilt seek in the moorland of Rannoch the
  wandering hero.

There is it, there, or in lofty Lochaber, where, silent
  upheaving,
Heaving from ocean to sky, and under snow-winds of
  September,
Visibly whitening at morn to darken by noon in the
  shining,
Rise on their mighty foundations the brethren huge of
  Ben Nevis?

There, or westward away, where roads are unknown to
    Loch Nevish,
And the great peaks look abroad over Skye to the west-
    ernmost islands?
There is it? there? or there? we shall find our wandering
    hero.

    Here, in Badenoch, here, in Lochaber anon, in
      Lochiel, in
Knoydart, Croydart, Moydart, Morrer, and Ardnamur-
    chan,
Here I see him, and here : I see him ; anon I lose him !
Even as cloud passing subtly unseen from mountain to
    mountain,
Leaving the crest of Ben More to be palpable next on
    Ben Vohrlich,
Or like to hawk of the hill which ranges and soars in its
    hunting,
Seen and unseen by turns, now here, now in ether
    eludent.

    Wherefore, like cloud of Ben More or hawk over-
      ranging the mountains,
Wherefore in Badenoch drear, in lofty Lochaber, Lochiel,
    and
Knoydart, Croydart, Moydart, Morrer, and Ardnamur-
    chan,
Wandereth he who should either with Adam be studying
    logic,
Or by the lochside of Rannoch on Katie his rhetoric using ;

He who, this three weeks past, past now long ago, to
the cottage
Punctual promised return to cares of classes and classics,
He who, smit to the heart by that youngest comeliest
daughter,
Bent, unregardful of spies, at her feet, spreading clothes
from her washtub?
Can it be with him through dreary Badenoch, Lochaber,
Lochiel and
Knoydart, Croydart, Moydart, Morrer, and Ardnamur-
chan,
Can it be with him he beareth the golden-haired lassie of
Rannoch?
This fierce, furious walking — o'er mountain-top and
moorland,
Sleeping in shieling and bothie, with drover on hillside
sleeping,
Folded in plaid, where sheep are strewn thicker than
rocks by Loch Awen,
This fierce, furious travel unwearying—cannot in truth be
Merely the wedding tour succeeding the week of wooing?

No, wherever be Katie, with Philip she is not; I see
him,
Lo, and he sitteth alone, and these are his words in the
mountains.
Souls of the dead, one fancies, can enter and be with
the living:
Would I were dead, I keep saying, that so I could go
and uphold her!

Spirits escaped from the body can enter and be with the living :

Entering unseen, and retiring unquestioned, they bring —do they feel too ?—

Joy, pure joy, as they mingle and mix inner essence with essence ;

Would I were dead, I keep saying, that so I could go and uphold her !

Joy, pure joy, bringing with them, and, when they retire, leaving after,

No cruel shame, no prostration, despondency ; memories rather,

Sweet happy hopes bequeathing. Ah ! wherefore not thus with the living ?

Would I were dead, I keep saying, that so I could go and uphold her !

Is it impossible, say you, these passionate fervent impulsions,

These projections of spirit to spirit, these inward embraces,

Should in strange ways, in her dreams, should visit her, strengthen her, shield her ?

Is it possible, rather, that these great floods of feeling

Setting in daily from me towards her should, impotent wholly,

Bring neither sound nor motion to that sweet shore they heave to ?

Efflux here, and there no stir nor pulse of influx !

It must reverberate surely, reverberate idly, it may be.

Yea, hath He set us our bounds which we shall not pass,
and cannot?
Would I were dead, I keep saying, that so I could go
and uphold her !

Surely, surely, when sleepless I lie in the mountain
lamenting,
Surely, surely, she hears in her dreams a voice, *I am with
thee*,
Saying, although not with thee; behold, for we mated
our spirits
Then, when we stood in the chamber, and knew not the
words we were saying;
Yea, if she felt me within her, when not with one finger
I touched her,
Surely she knows it, and feels it, while sorrowing here
in the moorland.
Would I were dead, I keep saying, that so I could go
and uphold her !

Spirits with spirits commingle and separate; lightly as
winds do,
Spice-laden South with the ocean-born zephyr ! they
mingle and sunder;
No sad remorses for them, no visions of horror and
vileness.
Elements fuse and resolve, as affinity draws and repels
them :
We, if we touch, must remain, if attracted, cohere to
the ending,

5

Guilty we are if we do not, and yet if we would we
    could not:
Would I were dead, I keep saying, that so I could go
    and uphold her!

    Surely the force that here sweeps me along in its
        violent impulse,
Surely my strength shall be in her, my help and pro-
    tection about her,
Surely in inner-sweet gladness and vigour of joy shall
    sustain her,
Till, the brief winter o'er-past, her own true sap in the
    springtide
Rise, and the tree I have bared be verduous e'en as
    aforetime!
Surely it may be, it should be, it must be. Yet, ever
    and ever,
Would I were dead, I keep saying, that so I could go
    and uphold her!

    No, wherever be Katie, with Philip she is not: behold,
        for
Here he is sitting alone, and these are his words in the
    mountain.

    And at the farm on the lochside of Rannoch, in parlour
        and kitchen,
Hark! there is music—yea, flowing of music, of milk,
    and of whisky;

Dancing and drinking, the young and the old, the spectators and actors,
Never not actors the young, and the old not alway
spectators:
Lo, I see piping and dancing! and whom in the midst of
the battle
Cantering loudly along there, or look you, with arms
uplifted,
Whistling, and snapping his fingers, and seizing his gay
smiling Janet,
Whom?—whom else but the Piper? the wary pre-
cognisant Piper,
Who, for the love of gay Janet, and mindful of old
invitation,
Putting it quite as a duty and urging grave claims to
attention,
True to his night had crossed over : there goeth he,
brimful of music,
Like to cork tossed by the eddies that foam under furious
lasher,
Like to skiff, lifted, uplifted, in lock, by the swift-swell-
ing sluices,
So with the music possessing him, swaying him, goeth
he, look you,
Swinging and flinging, and stamping and tramping, and
grasping and clasping
Whom but gay Janet?—Him rivalling, Hobbes, briefest-
kilted of heroes,
Enters, O stoutest, O rashest of creatures, mere fool of a
Saxon,

Skill-less of philabeg, skill-less of reel too, the whirl and
the twirl o't :
Him see I frisking and whisking, and ever at swifter
gyration
Under brief curtain revealing broad acres, not of broad-
cloth.
Him see I there and the Piper—the Piper what vision
beholds not ?
Him and His Honour with Arthur, with Janet our
Piper, and is it,
Is it, O marvel of marvels ! he too in the maze of the
mazy,
Skipping, and tripping, though stately, though languid,
with head on one shoulder,
Airlie, with sight of the Waistcoat the golden-haired
Katie consoling ?
Katie, who simple and comely, and smiling and blushing
as ever
What though she wear on that neck a blue kerchief
remembered as Philip's,
Seems in her maidenly freedom to need small console-
ment of waistcoats !—

Wherefore in Badenoch then, far away, in Lochaber,
Lochiel, in
Knoydart, Croydart, Moydart, Morrer, or Ardnamurchan,
Wanders o'er mountain and moorland, in shieling or
bothie is sleeping,
He, who,—and why should he not, then ? capricious ? or
is it rejected ?

Might to the piping of Rannoch be pressing the thrilling
    fair fingers,
Might, as he clasped her, transmit to her bosom the throb
    of his own—yea,—
Might in the joy of the reel be wooing and winning his
    Katie?

What is it Adam reads far off by himself in the cottage?
Reads yet again with emotion, again is preparing to
    answer?
Answered before too it had been, at once, on the spur of
    the moment,
Answered, but oft reconsidered, and afterthought needs
    will be spoken,
What is it Adam is reading? What was it Philip had
    written?

There was it writ, how Philip possessed undoubtedly
    had been,
Deeply, entirely possessed by the charm of the maiden of
    Rannoch ;
Deeply as never before ! how sweet and bewitching he
    felt her
Seen still before him at work, in the garden, the byre,
    the kitchen ;
How it was beautiful to him to stoop at her side in the
    shearing,
Binding uncouthly the ears that fell from her dexterous
    sickle,

Binding uncouthly the stooks, which she laid by her
    sickle to straighten;
How at the dance he had broken through shyness; for
    four days after
Lived on her eyes, unspeaking what lacked not articulate
    speaking;
How in the room where he slept he met her cleaning and
    dusting,
How he unmeaningly talked of clothes for the washing,—
    of this thing,
That thing, and still as he spoke felt folded into her, united,
Yea, without touch united, essentially, bodily with her,
Felt too that she too was feeling what he did.—Howbeit
    they parted.
How by a kiss from her lips he had seemed made nobler
    and stronger,
Yea, for the first time in life a man complete and perfect,
So forth! much that before too was heard of.—Howbeit
    they parted.

What had ended it all was singular, said he, very.—
I was walking along some two miles from the cottage,
Full of my dreamings—a girl went by in a party with
    others;
She had a cloak on, was stepping on quickly, for rain
    was beginning;
But as she passed, from the hood I saw her eyes look at
    me.
So quick a glance, so regardless I, that although I felt it,

You couldn't properly say our eyes met. She cast it, and
  left it :
It was three minutes, perhaps, ere I knew what it was.
  I had seen her,
Somewhere, before, I am sure, but that wasn't it : not
  its import :
No, it had seemed to regard me with simple superior
  insight,
Quietly saying to itself—Yes, there he is still in his fancy,
Letting drop from him at random as things not worth
  considering
All the benefits gathered and put in his hands by fortune,
Loosing a hold which others, contented and unambitious,
Trying down here to keep up, know the value of better
  than he does.
What is this?—was it perhaps?—Yes, there he is still in
  his fancy,
Doesn't yet see we have here just the things he is used to
  elsewhere ;
And that the things he likes here, elsewhere he wouldn't
  have looked at,
People here too are people, and not as fairy-land creatures;
He is in a trance, and possessed ; I wonder how long to
  continue ;
It is a shame and a pity—and no good likely to follow.—
—Something like this, but indeed I cannot the least
  define it,
Only, three hours thence I was off and away in the
  moorland,
Hiding myself from myself if I could ; the arrow within me.

Katie was not in the house, thank God : I saw her in
  passing,
Saw her, unseen myself, with the pang of a cruel deser-
  tion,
Poignant enough; which however but made me walk the
  faster,
Like a terrible spur running into one's vitals, and through
  them,
Turning me all into pain and sending me off, I suppose, like
One that is shot to the heart, and leaps in the air in his
  dying.
What dear Katie thinks, God knows ! poor child, may
  she only
Think me a fool and a madman, and no more worth her
  remembering !
Meantime all through the mountains I tramp and know
  not whither,
Tramp along here, and think, and know not what I should
  think.

  Tell me then, why, as I sleep amid hill-tops high in
  the moorland,
Still in my dreams I am pacing the streets of the dissolute
  city,
Where dressy girls slithering by upon pavements give
  sign for accosting,
Paint on their beautiless cheeks, and hunger and shame
  in their bosoms ;
Hunger by drink, and by that which they shudder, yet
  burn for, appeasing,—

Hiding their shame—ah God !—in the glare of the public
    gas-lights?
Why, while I feel my ears catching through slumber the
    run of the streamlet,
Still am I pacing the pavement, and seeing the sign for
    accosting,
Still am I passing those figures, not daring to look in
    their faces?
Why, when the chill, ere the light, of the daybreak
    uneasily wakes me,
Find I a cry in my heart crying up to the heaven of
    heavens,
No, Great Unjust Judge ! she is purity; I am the lost
    one.
No, I defy Thee, strike not ; crush me, if Thou wilt, who
    deserve it.

You will not think that I soberly look for such things
    for sweet Katie ;
Contemplate really, as possible even, a thing that would
    make one
Think death luxury, seek death, to get at damnation
    beyond it.
No, but the vision is on me; I now first see how it
    happens,
Feel how tender and soft is the heart of a girl; how
    passive
Fain would it be, how helpless ; and helplessness leads
    to destruction.

Maiden reserve, torn from off it, grows never again to
    reclothe it,
Modesty, broken through once, to immodesty flies for
    protection,
Desperate, braving when weakest the greatest and direst
    of dangers ;
Thinks to be bold and defiant at all times, cannot at all
    times,
Thinks by ignoring to fill up that breach which ignoring
    but widens.
Oh, who saws through the trunk, though he leave the
    tree up in the forest,
When the next wind casts it down, is *his* not the hand
    that smote it ?
Yea, and who barketh the tree, as he that felleth.

This is the answer, the second, which, pondering long
    with emotion,
There by himself in the cottage the Tutor addressed to
    Philip.

I was severe in my last, my dear Philip, and hasty ;
    forgive me ;
Yes, I was fain to reply ere I duly had read through
    your letter ;
But it was written in scraps with crossings and counter-
    crossings
Hard to connect with each other correctly, and hard to
    decipher ;

Paper was scarce, I suppose : forgive me : I write to
   console you.

  Grace is given of God, but knowledge is bought in the
   market ;
Knowledge needful for all, yet cannot be had for the
   asking.
There are exceptional beings, one finds them distant and
   rarely,
Who, endowed with the vision alike and the interpre-
   tation,
See, by the neighbours' eyes and their own still motions
   enlightened,
In the beginning the end, in the acorn the oak of the
   forest,
In the child of to-day its children to long generations,
In a thought or a wish a life, a drama, an epos.
There are inheritors, is it ; by mystical generation
Heiring the wisdom and ripeness of spirits gone by ;
   without labour
Owning what others by doing and suffering earn ; what
   old men
After long years of mistake and erasure are proud to
   have come to,
Sick with mistake and erasure possess when possession
   is idle.
Yes, there is power upon earth, seen feebly in women
   and children,
Which can, laying one hand on the cover, read off,
   unfaltering,

Leaf after leaf unlifted, the words of the closed book
　　under,
Words which we are poring at, hammering at, stumbling
　　at, spelling.
Rare is this ; to many in pittance and modicum given,
Working, an instinct blind, in woman and child and
　　rustic,
Rare in full measure, and often e'en then too maimed
　　and hampered ;
When with the power of speech, and the spirit united of
　　music,
Lo, a new day has dawned, and the ages wait upon
　　Shakespeare—
Rare is this ; wisdom mostly is bought for a price in the
　　market ;—
Rare is this ; and happy, who buys so much for so little,
As I conceive have you, and as I will hope has Katie.
Knowledge is needful for man,—needful no less for woman,
Even in Highland glens, were they vacant of shooter
　　and tourist.
Not that, of course, I mean to prefer your blindfold hurry
Unto a soul that abides most loving, yet most with-
　　holding ;
Least unfeeling though calm, self-contained yet most
　　unselfish ;
Renders help and accepts it, a man among men that are
　　brothers :
Views, not plucks, the beauty; adores, and demands no
　　embracing,
So in its peaceful passage whatever is lovely and gracious

Still, without seizing or spoiling, itself in itself reproducing.
No, I do not set Philip herein on the level of Arthur;
No, I do not compare still tarn with furious torrent,
Yet will the tarn overflow, assuaged in the lake be the
    torrent.

Women are weak, as you say, and love of all things to
    be passive,
Passive, patient, receptive, yea, even of wrong and mis-
    doing,
Even to force and misdoing with joy and victorious feeling
Patient, passive, receptive; for that is the strength of
    their being,
Like to the earth taking all things, and all to good con-
    verting.
Oh 'tis a snare indeed!—Moreover, remember it, Philip,
To the prestige of the richer the lowly are prone to be
    yielding,
Think that in dealing with them they are raised to a
    different region,
Where old laws and morals are modified, lost, exist not;
Ignorant they as they are, they have but to conform and
    be yielding.
There to protect and to guide them the old *'Tis not usual*
    avails not,
But of a new *'Tis not right* must the soul be with travail
    delivered,
Yea, itself of itself engender and bear the protector.
How shall a poor quiet girl self-create the law and com-
    mandment?

How shall a poor silly sheep get endowed with the will
of a woman?

But I said this in my letter before, and need not
repeat it.
You will have seen yourself the danger of pantry flirta-
tion,
You will not now run after what merely attracts and
entices,
Every-day things highly coloured, and commonplace
carved and gilded:
You will henceforth seek only the good; and seek it,
Philip,
Where it is—not more abundant, perhaps, but more
easily met with;
Where you are surer to find it, less likely to run into
error,
In your station; regardful of that, though not dependent.
But as I said, I have said this before, and need not
repeat it.

So was the letter completed: a postscript afterward
added,
Telling the tale that was told by the dancers returning
from Rannoch.
So was the letter completed: but query, whither to
send it?
Not for the will-of-the-wisp, the cloud, and the hawk of
the moorland,

Ranging afar through Lochaber, Lochiel, and Knoydart, and Croydart,
Have even latest extensions adjusted a postal arrangement.
Query resolved very shortly, when Hope, from his chamber descending,
Came with a note in his hand from the Lady, his aunt, of Ilay;
Came and revealed the contents of a missive that brought strange tidings;
Came and announced to the friends, in a voice that was husky with wonder,
Philip was staying at Balloch, was there in the room with the Countess,
Philip to Balloch had come, and was dancing with Lady Maria.

Philip at Balloch, he said, after all that stately refusal,
He there at last—O strange ! O marvel, marvel of marvels !
Airlie, the Waistcoat, with Katie, we left him this morning at Rannoch ;
Airlie with Katie, he said, and Philip with Lady Maria.

And amid laughter Adam paced up and down, repeating
Over and over, unconscious, the phrase which Hope had lent him,
Dancing at Balloch, you say, in the Castle, with Lady Maria.

Entering and through door on her left, and she, in fine
and Chevette.

Pierre on his return passed just a little unexpected,
dark, freckled, and very lovely, and withdrew from the
gentle descendant.

Come with a note in his hope—said the Dauphin, a
or ...

said and smoked Chocolate of ... munch and thought
in the distance.

Pierre and concerned in the faintly, it was the saying—
me, to walk with.

Pelle ... taught to Barcelona—so there was a cave,
... and understand, the ...

Pelle ... which had been ... was digging and ...
world.

Pelle of the ... banner of ... only stopped about
the lower ... the Queen ... Queen ... and making
survive.

Barre, to ... concerned with discovery such ... the ...
of ... his Richard.

smile with which he said, and the figure of leg, Marie.

Pelle said, Madame, quietly, and if it were mean,
said she.

Over many ... concerning ... These ... this they
said he.

Pointing at Pelle, you say, to the ladies, did I say
Marie.

V.

. . . Putavi
Stultus ego huic nostræ similem.

V.

So in the cottage with Adam the pupils five together
Duly remained, and read, and looked no more for
Philip,
Philip at Balloch shooting, and dancing with Lady
Maria.
Breakfast at eight, and now, for brief September day-
light,
Luncheon at two, and dinner at seven, or even later,
Five full hours between for the loch and the glen and the
mountain,—
So in the joy of their life and the glory of shooting-
jackets,
So they read and roamed, the pupils five with Adam.

What if autumnal shower came frequent and chill from
the westward,
What if on browner sward with yellow leaves besprinkled,
Gemming the crispy blade, the delicate gossamer gem-
ming,
Frequent and thick lay at morning the chilly beads of
hoar-frost,
Duly in matutine still, and daily, whatever the weather,

Bathed in the rain and the frost and the mist, with the
  Glory of Headers,
Hope. Thither also at times, of cold and of possible
  gutters
Careless, unmindful, unconscious, would Hobbes, or ere
  they departed,
Come, in heavy pea-coat his trouserless trunk en-
  wrapping,
Come, under coat over-brief those lusty legs displaying,
All from the shirt to the slipper the natural man reveal-
  ing.

  Duly there they bathed, and daily, the twain or the
    trio,
There where of mornings was custom, where over a ledge
  of granite
Into a granite basin descended the amber torrent ;
Beautiful, very, to gaze in ere plunging ; beautiful also,
Perfect as picture, as vision entrancing that comes to the
  sightless,
Through the great granite jambs the stream, and glen,
  and mountain,
Purple with heather the mountain, the level stream in
  foreground ;
Beautiful, seen by snatches in intervals of dressing,
Morn after morn, unsought for, recurring ; themselves
  too seeming
Not as spectators, accepted into it, immingled, as truly
Part of it as are the kine in the field lying there by the
  birches.

So they bathed, they read, they roamed in glen and
    forest;
Far amid blackest pines to the waterfalls they shadow,
Far up the long, long glen to the loch, and the loch
    beyond it,
Deep, under huge red cliffs, a secret; and oft by the
    starlight,
Or the aurora, perchance, racing home for the eight
    o'clock mutton.
So they bathed, and read, and roamed in heathery High-
    land;
There, in the joy of their life and glory of shooting-
    jackets,
Bathed and read and roamed, and looked no more for
    Philip.

List to a letter that came from Philip at Balloch to
    Adam.

I am here, O my friend!—idle, but learning wisdom.
Doing penance, you think; content, if so, in my
    penance.
You have conjectured a change must have come to my
    mind: I believe it!
You will believe it too, if I tell you the thoughts that
    haunt me!

Often I find myself saying, while watching in dance or
    on horseback

One that is here, in her freedom and grace, and imperial
    sweetness,
Often I find myself, saying, old faith and doctrine
    abjuring,
Into the crucible casting philosophies, facts, convictions,—

Were it not well that the stem should be naked of leaf
    and of tendril,
Poverty-stricken, the barest, the dismallest stick of the
    garden ;
Flowerless, leafless, unlovely, for ninety-and-nine long
    summers,
So in the hundredth, at last, were bloom for one day at
    the summit,
So but that fleeting flower were lovely as Lady Maria.

Often I find myself saying, and know not myself as I
    say it,
What of the poor and the weary? their labour and pain
    is needed.
Perish the poor and the weary ! what can they better
    than perish,
Perish in labour for her, who is worth the destruction of
    empires !
What ? for a mite, for a mote, an impalpable odour of
    honour,
Armies shall bleed ; cities burn ; and the soldier red
    from the storming
Carry hot rancour and lust into chambers of mothers and
    daughters ?

What! would ourselves for the cause of an hour en-
counter the battle,
Slay and be slain; lie rotting in hospital, hulk, and
prison :
Die as a dog dies; die, secure that to uttermost ages
Not one ray shall illumine our midnight of shame and
dishonour,
Yea, till in silence the fingers stand still in the world's
great dial,
Fathers and mothers, the gentle and good of unborn
generations,
Shall to their little ones point out our names for their
loathing and horror ?
Yea,—and shall hodmen in beer-shops complain of a
glory denied them
Which could not ever be theirs more than now it is theirs
as spectators ?
Which could not be, in all earth, if it were not for labour
of hodmen ?

And I find myself saying, and what I am saying dis-
cern not,
Dig in thy deep dark prison, O miner! and finding be
thankful ;
Though, unpolished by thee, unto thee unseen in per-
fection,
While thou art eating black bread in the poisonous air of
thy cavern,
Far away glitter the gem on the peerless neck of a
Princess,

Dig, and starve, and be thankful; it is so, and thou hast
  been aiding.

Often I find myself saying, in irony is it, or earnest?

Yea, what is more, be rich, O ye rich! be sublime in
  great houses,
Purple and delicate linen endure; be of Burgundy
  patient;
Suffer that service be done you, permit of the page and
  the valet,
Vex not your souls with annoyance of charity-schools or
  of districts,
Cast not to swine of the sty the pearls that should gleam
  in your foreheads.
Live, be lovely, forget them, be beautiful even to proudness,
Even for their poor sakes whose happiness is to behold
  you;
Live, be uncaring, be joyous, be sumptuous; only be
  lovely,—
Sumptuous not for display, and joyous, not for enjoyment;
Not for enjoyment truly; for Beauty, and God's great
  glory!

Yes, and I say, and it seems inspiration—of good or
  evil!
Is it not He that hath done it, and who shall dare gain-
  say it?

Is it not even of Him, who hath made us? Yea, for the lions,
Roaring after their prey, do seek their meat from God !
Is it not even of Him, who one kind over another
All the works of His hand hath disposed in a wonderful
    order ?
Who hath made man, as the beasts, to live the one on
    the other,
Who hath made man as Himself to know the law—and
    accept it !
You will wonder at this, my friend ! I also wonder,
But we must live and learn ; we can't know all things at
    twenty.

List to a letter of Hobbes to Philip his friend at
    Balloch :

All Cathedrals are Christian, all Christians are Cathe-
    drals,—
Such is the orthodox doctrine ; 'tis ours with a slight
    variation ;
Every woman is, or ought to be, a Cathedral,
Built on the ancient plan, a Cathedral pure and perfect,
Built by that only law, that Use be suggester of Beauty,
Nothing concealed that is done, but all things done to
    adornment,
Meanest abilities seized as occasions to grace and em-
    bellish.—

So had I duly commenced in the spirit and style of my
    Philip,

So had I formally opened the Treatise upon the *Laws of
Architectural Beauty in Application to Women*,
So had I writ.—But my fancies are palsied by tidings
they tell me :
Tidings—ah me, can it be then ? that I, the blasphemer
accounted,
Here am with reverent heed at the wondrous analogy
working,
Pondering thy words and thy gestures, whilst thou, a
prophet apostate,
(How are the mighty fallen !) whilst thou, a shepherd
travestie,
(How are the mighty fallen !) with gun,—with pipe no
longer,
Teachest the woods to re-echo thy game-killing recanta-
tions,
Teachest thy verse to exalt Amaryllis, a Countess'
daughter ?

What, thou forgettest, bewildered, my master, that
rightly considered
Beauty must ever be useful, what truly is useful is graceful?
She that is handy is handsome, good dairy-maids must be
good-looking,
If but the butter be nice, the tournure of the elbow is
shapely,
If the cream-cheeses be white, far whiter the hands that
made them,
If—but alas, is it true? while the pupil alone in the
cottage

Slowly elaborates here thy system of feminine graces,
Thou in the palace, its author, art dining, small-talking,
    dancing,
Dancing and pressing the fingers kid-gloved of a Lady
    Maria !

These are the final words, that came to the Tutor from
    Balloch.
Yes, you have conquered, my friend ! you will meet me,
    I hope, in Oxford,
Altered in manners and mind.   I yield to the laws and
    arrangements,
Yield to the ancient existent decrees : who am I to resist
    them ?
Yes, you will find me altered in mind, I think, as in
    manners,
Anxious too to atone for six weeks' loss of your logic.

So in the cottage with Adam, the pupils five together,
Read, and bathed, and roamed, and thought not now of
    Philip,
All in the joy of their life, and glory of shooting-jackets.

VI.

Ducite ab urbe domum, mea carmina, ducite
Daphnin.

VI.

Bright October was come, the misty-bright October,
Bright October was come to burn and glen and cottage ;
But the cottage was empty, the matutine deserted.

Who are these that walk by the shore of the salt sea
water ?
Here in the dusky eve, on the road by the salt sea water?

Who are these? and where? it is no sweet seclusion ;
Blank hill-sides slope down to a salt sea-loch at their
bases,
Scored by runnels, that fringe ere they end with rowan
and alder ;
Cottage here and there outstanding bare on the mountain,
Peat-roofed, windowless, white ; the road underneath by
the water.

There on the blank hill-side, looking down through the
loch to the ocean,
There with a runnel beside, and pine trees twain before it,
There with the road underneath, and in sight of coaches
and steamers,

Dwelling of David Mackaye and his daughters Elspie
and Bella,
Send us up a column of smoke the Bothie of Toper-na-
fuosich.

And of the elder twain the elder was telling the
younger,
How on his pittance of soil he lived, and raised
potatoes,
Barley and oats, in the bothie where lived his father
before him ;
Yet was smith by trade, and had travelled making horse-
shoes
Far, in the army had seen some service with brave Sir
Hector,
Wounded soon, and discharged, disabled as smith and
soldier ;
He had been many things since that,—drover, school-
master,
Whitesmith,—but when his brother died childless came
up hither ;
And although he could get fine work that would pay, in
the city,
Still was fain to abide where his father abode before
him.
And the lasses are bonnie,—I'm father and mother to
them,—
Bonnie and young ; they're healthier here, I judge, and
safer :
I myself find time for their reading, writing, and learning.

So on the road they walk, by the shore of the salt sea
    water ;
Silent a youth and a maid, and elders twain conversing.

This was the letter that came when Adam was leaving
    the cottage :
If you can manage to see me before going off to Dartmoor,
Come by Tuesday's coach through Glencoe (you have not
    seen it),
Stop at the ferry below, and ask your way (you will
    wonder,
There however I am) to the Bothie of Toper-na-fuosich.

And on another scrap, of next day's date, was written :
It was by accident purely I lit on the place ; I was going
Quietly travelling homeward, by one of these wretched
    coaches ;
One of the horses cast a shoe ; and a farmer passing
Said, Old David's your man ; a clever fellow at shoeing
Once ; just up by the firs ; they call it Toper-na-fuosich.
So I saw and spoke with David Mackaye, our acquaint-
    ance.
When we came to the journey's end, some five miles
    further,
In my unoccupied evening I walked back again to the
    bothie.

But on a final crossing, still later in date was added:
Come as soon as you can ; be sure and do not miss
    me.

7

Who would have guessed I should find my haven and
    end of travel,
Here, by accident, too, in the bothie we laughed about so?
Who would have guessed that here would be she whose
    glance at Rannoch
Turned me in that mysterious way; yes, angels conspiring,
Slowly drew me, conducted me, home, to herself; the
    needle
Which in the shaken compass flew hither and thither, at
    last, long
Quivering, ,poises to north—I think so.   But I am
    cautious;
More, far more, than I was in the old silly days when
    I left you.
Though I much fear that my eyes may betray me.   Still
    I am heedful.—
Any way try,—and have learnt some self-control of
    manner,
As I conceive, with staying and contemplating at Balloch;
Other things I hope, but, clearly, to be more retentive.

    Not at the bothie now; at the changehouse in the
      clachan;
Why I delay my letter is more than I can tell you.

    There was another scrap, without date or comment,
Dotted over with various observations, as follows:
Only think, I had danced with her twice, and did not
    remember.

I was as one that sleeps on the railway; one, who
    dreaming
Hears through his dream the name of his home shouted
    out; hears and hears not,—
Faint and louder again, and less loud, dying in distance;
Dimly conscious, with something of inward debate and
    choice,—and
Sense of claim and reality present, relapses
Nevertheless, and continues the dream and fancy, while
    forward
Swiftly, remorseless, the car presses on, he knows not
    whither.

    Handsome who handsome is, who handsome does is
    more so;
Pretty is all very pretty, it's prettier far to be useful.
No, fair Lady Maria, I say not that; but I *will* say,
Stately is service accepted, but lovelier service rendered,
Interchange of service the law and condition of beauty:
Any way beautiful only to be the thing one is meant
    for.
I, I am sure, for the sphere of mere ornament am not
    intended:
No, nor she, I think, thy sister at Toper-na-fuosich;
No, she transcends it far, as I perhaps fall below it.

    This was the letter of Philip, and this had brought the
    Tutor.
This is why tutor and pupil are walking with David and
    Elspie.

When for the night they part, and these, once more
together,
Went by the lochside along to the changehouse near in
the clachan,
Thus to his pupil anon commences the grave man Adam :

Yes, she is beautiful, Philip, beautiful even as morning :
Yes, it is that which I said, the good and not the
attractive !
Happy is he that finds, and finding does not leave it !

And by his side in silence walked Philip, and presently
answered,
Happy is he that finds, if he lose not: but happy, and
more too,
Blessed, be he by whose showing the seeker is changed
to the finder.

Ten more days did Adam with Philip abide at the
changehouse,
Ten more nights they met, they walked with father and
daughter.
Ten more nights, and night by night more distant away
were
Philip and she ; every night less heedful, by habit, the
father.
Happy ten days, most happy ; and, otherwise than
thought of,
Fortunate visit of Adam, companion and friend to David.

Happy ten days, be ye fruitful of happiness! Pass o'er
  them slowly,
Slowly; like cruise of the prophet be multiplied, even to
  ages!
Pass slowly o'er them, ye days of October; ye soft misty
  mornings,
Long dusky eves; pass slowly; and thou, great Term-
  time of Oxford,
Awful with lectures and books, and Little-Goes and
  Great-Goes,
Till but the sweet bud be perfect, recede and retire for
  the lovers,
Yea, for the sweet love of lovers, postpone thyself even
  to doomsday!
Pass o'er them slowly, ye hours; be with them, ye Loves
  and Graces!

  Indirect and evasive no longer, a cowardly bather,
Clinging to bough and to rock, and sidling along by the
  edges,
In your faith, ye Muses and Graces, who love the plain
  present,
Scorning historic abridgment and artifice anti-poetic,
In your faith, ye Muses and Loves, ye Loves and Graces,
I will confront the great peril, and speak with the mouth
  of the lovers,
As they spoke by the alders, at evening, the runnel below
  them,
Elspie a diligent knitter, and Philip her fingers watching.

VII.

Vesper adest, juvenes, consurgite; Vesper Olympo
Expectata diu vix tandem lumina tollit.

For she confessed, as they sat in the dusk, and he saw
    not her blushes,
Elspie confessed at the sports long ago with her father
    she saw him,
When at the door the old man had told him the name of
    the bothie :
There after that at the dance; yet again at the dance in
    Rannoch —
And she was silent, confused. Confused much rather,
    Philip
Buried his face in his hands, his face that with blood was
    bursting.
Silent, confused, yet by pity she conquered her fear, and
    continued.

Katie is good and not silly : be comforted, sir, about her ;
Katie is good and not silly; tender, but not like many
Carrying off, and at once for fear of being seen, in the
    bosom
Locking up as in a cupboard the pleasure that any man
    gives them,
Keeping it out of sight as a prize they need be ashamed of ;
That is the way, I think, sir, in England more than in
    Scotland ;
No, she lives and takes pleasure in all, as in beautiful
    weather,

Sorry to lose it, but just as we would be to lose fine
    weather.
And she is strong to return to herself, and feel undeserted,
For she always keeps burning a cheerful fire inside her.
Oh, she is strong, and not silly; she thinks no more
    about you;
She has had kerchiefs before from gentle, I know, as from
    simple.
Yes, she is good and not silly: yet were you wrong,
    Mr. Philip,
Wrong, for yourself perhaps more than for her.

                          But Philip replied not.
Raised not his eyes from the hands on his knees.

                        And Elspie continued:
That was what gave me much pain, when I met you that
    dance at Rannoch,
Dancing myself too with you, while Katie danced with
    Donald;
That was what gave me such pain; I thought it all
    delusion,
All a mere chance, and accident,—not proper choosing,—
There were at least five or six—not there, no, that I
    don't say,
But in the country about,—you might just as well have
    been courting.
That was what gave me much pain, and (you won't
    remember that, though)
Three days after, I met you, beside my uncle's, walking.

And I was wondering much, and hoped you wouldn't
  notice,
So as I passed I couldn't help looking. You didn't
  know me.
But I was glad when I heard, next day, you were gone
  to the teacher.

  And uplifting his face, at last, with eyes dilated,
Large as great stars in mist, and dim with dabbled lashes,
Philip with new tears starting,

                              You think I do not remember,
Said, suppose that I did not observe! Ah me, shall I
  tell you?
Elspie, it was your look that sent me away from Rannoch.
It was your glance that, descending, an instant reve-
  lation,
Showed me where I was, and whitherward going; re-
  called me,
Sent me, not to my books, but to wrestlings of thought
  in the mountains,
Yes, I have carried your glance within me, undimmed,
  unaltered,
As a lost boat the compass some passing ship has lent
  her,
Many a weary mile on road, and hill, and moorland:
It has been with me in shieling and bothie of wandering
  drovers,
It has been with me, more precious, in chariot and
  palace of peeress:

O, did the sailor bewildered observe when they told him
    his bearings?
O, did he cast overboard, when they parted, the compass
    they gave him?

    And he continued more firmly, although with stronger
       emotion :
Elspie, why should I speak it? you cannot believe it,
    and should not :
Why should I say that I love, which I all but said to
    another?
Yet, should I dare,—should I say: O Elspie, you only I
    love ; you,
First and sole in my life that has been and surely that
    shall be,
Could—O, could you believe it, O Elspie, believe it and
    spurn not,
Is it possible—possible, Elspie?

                 Well,—she answered,
Quietly, after her fashion, still knitting,—Well, I think
    of it.
Yes,—I don't know, Mr. Philip,—but only it feels to me
    strangely
Like to the high new bridge they used to build at, below
    there,
Over the burn and glen on the road. You won't under-
    stand me,
But I keep saying in my mind,—this long time slowly
    with trouble

I have been building myself up, up, and toilfully raising,
Just like as if the bridge were to do itself without masons,
Painfully getting myself upraised one stone on another,
All one side I mean ; and now I see on the other
Just such another fabric uprising, better and stronger,
Close to me, coming to join me : and then, I sometimes
    fancy,—
Sometimes I find myself dreaming at nights about arches
    and bridges,—
Sometimes I dream of a great invisible hand coming
    down, and
Dropping the great key-stone in the middle : there in my
    dreaming,
There I feel the great key-stone coming in, and through it
Feel the other part—all the other stones of the archway,
Joined into mine with a queer happy sense of complete-
    ness, tingling
All the way up from the other side's basement-stones in
    the water,
Through the very grains of mine :—Just like, when the
    steel, that you showed us
Moved to the magnet, it seemed a feeling got hold of
    them both.—But
This is confusion and nonsense. I am mixing all things
    I can think of,
And you won't understand me, Mr. Philip.

                  But while she was speaking,
So it happened, a moment she paused from her work,
    and pondering,

Laid her hand on her lap: Philip took it, she did not
  resist :
So he retained her fingers, the knitting being stopped.
  But emotion
Came all over her more and more, from his hand, from her
  heart, and
Most from the sweet idea and image her brain was
  renewing.
So he retained her hand, and, his tears down dropping
  on it,
Trembling a long time kissed it at last.   And she
  ended:
And, as she ended, up rose he, saying: What have I
  heard?   Oh,
What have I done, that such words should be said to me?
  Oh, I see it,
See the great key-stone coming down from the heaven
  of heavens !
And he fell at her feet, and buried his face in her apron.

  But as under the moon and stars they went to the
  cottage,
Elspie sighed and said, Be patient, dear Mr. Philip,
Do not do anything hasty.   It is all so soon, so sudden,
Do not say anything yet to any one.

                                    Elspie, he answered,
Does not my friend go on Friday?   I then shall see
  nothing of you ;
Do not I go myself on Monday?

But oh, he said, Elspie,
Do as I bid you, my child; do not go on calling me
    Mr. ;
Might I not just as well be calling you Miss Elspie?
Call me, this heavenly night, for once, for the first time,
    Philip !
Philip, she said, and laughed, and said she could not
    say it ;
Philip, she said ; he turned, and kissed the sweet lips as
    they said it.

But on the morrow Elspie kept out of the way of
    Philip ;
And at the evening seat when he took her hand by the
    alders,
Drew it back, saying, almost peevishly,

No, Mr. Philip,
I was quite right, last night ; it is too soon, too sudden.
What I told you before was foolish perhaps, and hasty :
When I think it over, I am shocked and terrified at it.
Not that at all I unsay it ; that is, I know I said it,
And when I said it, felt it.   But oh, we must wait, Mr.
    Philip !
We mustn't pull ourselves at the great key-stone of the
    centre ;
Some one else up above must hold it, fit it, and fix it ;
If we try to do it, we shall only damage the archway,
Damage all our own work that we wrought, our painful
    upbuilding.

When, you remember, you took my hand last evening,
     talking,
I was all over a tremble: and as you pressed the
     fingers
After, and afterwards kissed it, I could not speak. And
     then, too,
As we went home, you kissed me for saying your name.
     It was dreadful.
I have been kissed before, she added, blushing slightly,
I have been kissed more than once by Donald, my
     cousin, and others ;
It is the way of the lads, and I make up my mind not to
     mind it ;
But, Mr. Philip, last night, and from you, it was
     different, quite, sir.
When I think all that over, I am shocked and terrified
     at it.
Yes, it is dreadful to me.

                    She paused, but quickly continued ;
Smiling almost fiercely, continued, looking upward:
You are too strong, you see, Mr. Philip! You are like
     the sea there,
Which *will* come, through the straits and all between
     the mountains,
Forcing its great strong tide into every nook and inlet,
Getting far in, up the quiet streams of sweet inland
     water,
Sucking it up, and stopping it, turning it, driving it
     backward,

Quite preventing its own quiet running. And then, soon after,
Back it goes off, leaving weeds on the shore, and wrack and uncleanness :
And the poor burn in the glen tries again its peaceful running,
But it is brackish and tainted, and all its banks disordered.
That was what I dreamt all last night.   I was the burnie,
Trying to get along through the tyrannous brine, and could not,
I was confined and squeezed in the coils of the great salt tide, that
Would mix in itself with me, and change me; I felt myself changing;
And I struggled, and screamed, I believe, in my dream. It was dreadful.
You are too strong, Mr. Philip! I am but a poor slender burnie,
Used to the glens and the rocks, the rowan and birch of the woodies,
Quite unused to the great salt sea; quite afraid and unwilling.

Ere she had spoken two words had Philip released her fingers;
As she went on, he recoiled, fell back, and shook, and shivered;
There he stood, looking pale and ghastly; when she had ended,

Answering in hollow voice,

It is true; oh, quite true, Elspie.
Oh, you are always right; oh, what, what have I been
doing?
I will depart to-morrow.   But oh, forget me not wholly,
Wholly, Elspie, nor hate me, no, do not hate me, my
Elspie.

But a revulsion passed through the brain and bosom
of Elspie,
And she got up from her seat on the rock, putting by
her knitting;
Went to him, where he stood, and answered,

No, Mr. Philip,
No, you are good, Mr. Philip, and gentle; and I am
the foolish,
No, Mr. Philip; forgive me.

She stepped right to him, and boldly
Took up his hand, and placed it in hers; he daring no
movement,
Took up the cold hanging hand, upforcing the heavy
elbow.
I am afraid, she said, but I will! and kissed the fingers.
And he fell on his knees, and kissed her own past
counting.

But a revulsion wrought in the brain and bosom of
Elspie;

And the passion she just had compared to the vehement
  ocean,
Urging in high spring-tide its masterful way through the
  mountains,
Forcing and flooding the silvery stream, as it runs from
  the inland ;
That great river withdrawn, receding here and passive,
Felt she in myriad spring, her sources, far in the
  mountains,
Stirring, collecting, rising, upheaving, forth outflowing,
Taking and joining, right welcome, that delicate rill in
  the valley,
Filling it, making it strong, and still descending, seeking,
With a blind forefeeling descending, evermore seeking,
With a delicious forefeeling, the great still sea before
  it ;
There deep into it, far, to carry, and lose in its bosom,
Waters that still from their sources exhaustless are fain
  to be added.

As he was kissing her fingers, and knelt on the ground
  . before her,
Yielding backward she sank to her seat, and of what she
  was doing
Ignorant, bewildered, in sweet multitudinous vague
  emotion,
Stooping, knowing not what, put her lips to the curl on
  his forehead ;
And Philip raising himself, gently, for the first time
  round her,

Passing his arms, close, close, enfolded her, close to his
    bosom.

As they went home by the moon, Forgive me, Philip,
    she whispered,
I have so many things to think of, all of a sudden;
I who had never once thought a thing,—in my ignorant
    Highlands.

VIII.

Jam veniet virgo, jam dicetur hymenæus,
Hymen, O hymenæe! Hymen, ades, O hymenæe!

VIII.

But a revulsion again came over the spirit of Elspie,
When she thought of his wealth, his birth and education:
Wealth indeed but small, though to her a difference
    truly;
Father nor mother had Philip, a thousand pounds his
    portion,
Somewhat impaired in a world where nothing is had for
    nothing;
Fortune indeed but small, and prospects plain and simple.

But the many things that he knew, and the ease of a
    practised
Intellect's motion, and all those indefinable graces
(Were they not hers too, Philip?) of speech, and manner,
    and movement,
Lent by the knowledge of self, and wisely instructed
    feeling,—
When she thought of all these, and these contemplated
    daily,
Daily appreciating more, and more exactly appraising,—
With these thoughts, and the terror withal of a thing she
    could not

Estimate, and of a step (such a step !) in the dark to be
    taken,
Terror nameless and ill-understood of deserting her
    station,—
Daily heavier, heavier upon her pressed the sorrow,
Daily distincter, distincter within her arose the conviction,
He was too high, too perfect, and she so unfit, so
    unworthy,
(Ah me ! Philip, that ever a word such as that should be
    written !)
It would not do for him; nor for her; she also was
    something,
Not much indeed, and different, yet not to be lightly
    extinguished.
Should *he—he*, have a wife beneath him ? herself be
An inferior there where only equality can be ?
It would be neither for him nor for her.

                                        Alas for Philip !
Many were tears and great was perplexity. Nor had
    availed then
All his prayer and all his device.

                            But much was spoken
Now, between Adam and Elspie : companions were they
    hourly :
Much by Elspie to Adam, inquiring, anxiously seeking,
From his experience seeking impartial accurate statement
What it was to do this or do that, go hither or thither,

How in the after-life would seem what, now seeming
    certain,
Might so soon be reversed; in her quest and obscure
    exploring
Still from that quiet orb soliciting light to her foot-
    steps;
Much by Elspie to Adam, inquiringly, eagerly seeking:
Much by Adam to Elspie, informing, reassuring,
Much that was sweet to Elspie, by Adam heedfully
    speaking,
Quietly, indirectly, in general terms, of Philip,
Gravely, but indirectly, not so incognisant wholly,
But as suspending until she should seek it, direct in-
    timation;
Much that was sweet in her heart of what he was and
    would be,
Much that was strength to her mind, confirming beliefs
    and insights
Pure and unfaltering, but young and mute and timid for
    action:
Much of relations of rich and poor, and of true education.

It was on Saturday eve, in the gorgeous bright October,
Then when brackens are changed, and heather blooms
    are faded,
And amid russet of heather and fern green trees are
    bonnie;
Alders are green, and oaks; the rowan scarlet and
    yellow;
One great glory of broad gold pieces appears the aspen,

And the jewels of gold that were hung in the hair of the
　　birch-tree,
Pendulous, here and there, her coronet, necklace, and
　　earrings,
Cover her now, o'er and o'er; she is weary and scatters
　　them from her.
Then upon Saturday eve, in the gorgeous bright October,
Under the alders knitting, gave Elspie her troth to
　　Philip.

　　For, as they talked, anon she said,—
　　　　　　　　　　　　　　It is well, Mr. Philip,
Yes, it is well: I have spoken, and learnt a deal with
　　the teacher.
At the last I told him all, I could not help it :
And it came easier with him than could have been with
　　my father ;
And he calmly approved, as one that had fully considered.
Yes, it is well, I have hoped, though quite too great and
　　sudden ;
I am so fearful, I think it ought not to be for years yet.
I am afraid ; but believe in you ; and I trust to the
　　teacher ;
You have done all things gravely and temperate, not as
　　in passion ;
And the teacher is prudent, and surely can tell what is
　　likely.
What my father will say, I know not; we will obey him:
But for myself, I could dare to believe all well, and venture.
O Mr. Philip, may it never hereafter seem to be different!

And she hid her face—
        Oh, where, but in Philip's bosom !

  After some silence, some tears too perchance, Philip
    laughed, and said to her,
So, my own Elspie, at last you are clear that I'm bad
    enough for you.
Ah ! but your father won't make one half the question
    about it
You have—he'll think me, I know, nor better nor worse
    than Donald,
Neither better nor worse for my gentlemanship and
    bookwork,
Worse, I fear, as he knows me an idle and vagabond
    fellow,
Though he allows,—but he'll think it was all for your
    sake, Elspie,—
Though he allows I did some good at the end of the
    shearing.
But I had thought in Scotland you didn't care for this folly.
How I wish, he said, you had lived all your days in the
    Highlands !
This is what comes of the year you spent in our foolish
    England.
You do not all of you feel these fancies.

                No, she answered,
And in her spirit the freedom and ancient joy was
    reviving.
No, she said, and uplifted herself, and looked for her
    knitting,

No, nor do *I*, dear Philip, I don't myself feel always
As I have felt, more sorrow for me, these four days lately,
Like the Peruvian Indians I read about last winter,
Out in America there, in somebody's Life of Pizarro;
Who were as good perhaps as the Spaniards; only weaker;
And that the one big tree might spread its roots and
     branches,
All the lesser about it must even be felled and perish,
No, I feel much more as if I, as well as you, were,
Somewhere, a leaf on the one great tree, that, up from
     old time
Growing, contains in itself the whole of the virtue and
     life of
Bygone days, drawing now to itself all kindreds and
     nations,
And must have for itself the whole world for its root and
     branches.
No, I belong to the tree, I shall not decay in the shadow;
Yes, and I feel the life-juices of all the world and the ages,
Coming to me as to you, more slowly no doubt and
     poorer:
You are more near, but then you will help to convey
     them to me.
No, don't smile, Philip, now, so scornfully!—While you
     look so
Scornful and strong, I feel as if I were standing and
     trembling,
Fancying the burn in the dark a wide and rushing river;
And I feel coming into me from you, or it may be from
     elsewhere,

Strong contemptuous resolve ; I forget, and I bound as
  across it.
But after all, you know, it may be a dangerous river.

  Oh, if it were so, Elspie, he said, I can carry you over.
Nay, she replied, you would tire of having me for a
  burden.
O sweet burden, he said, and are you not light as a
  feather ?
But it is deep, very likely, she said, over head and ears
  too.

  O, let us try, he answered, the waters themselves will
  support us,
Yea, very ripples and waves will form to a boat under-
  neath us ;
There is a boat, he said, and a name is written upon it,
Love, he said, and kissed her—

            But I will read your books, though,
Said she, you'll leave me some, Philip?

            Not I, replied he, a volume.
This is the way with you all, I perceive, high and low
  together.
Women must read, as if they didn't know all beforehand :
Weary of plying the pump, we turn to the running water,
And the running spring will needs have a pump built on it.
Weary and sick of our books, we come to repose in your
  eye-sight,

As to the woodland and water, the freshness and beauty
 of Nature.
Lo, you will talk, forsooth, of things we are sick to death
 of.

What, she said, and if I have let you become my
 sweetheart,
I am to read no books ! but you may go your ways then,
And I will read, she said, with my father at home as I
 used to.

If you must have it, he said, I myself will read them
 to you.

Well, she said, but no, I will read to myself, when I
 choose it.
What, you suppose we never read anything here in our
 Highlands,
Bella and I with the father, in all our winter evenings !
But we must go, Mr. Philip—

      I shall not go at all, said
He, if you call me Mr.   Thank Heaven ! that's well over.

No, but it's not, she said, it is not over, nor will be,
Was it not, then, she asked, the name I called you first
 by ?
No, Mr. Philip, no—you have kissed me enough for two
 nights ;
No—come, Philip, come, or I'll go myself without you.

You never call me Philip, he answered, until I kiss you.

As they went home by the moon that, waning, now
　　rose later;
Stepping through mossy stones by the runnel under the
　　alders,
Loitering unconsciously: Philip, she said, I will not be a
　　lady;
We will do work together—you do not wish me a lady.
It is a weakness perhaps, and a foolishness; still it is
　　so;
I could not bear to sit and be waited on by footmen,
No, not even by women—

　　　　　　　　　And God forbid, he answered,
God forbid you should ever be aught but yourself, my
　　Elspie!
As for service, I love it not, I; your weakness is mine
　　too,
I am sure Adam told you as much as that about me.

I am sure, she said, he called you wild and flighty.
That was true, he said, till my wings were clipped by
　　Elspie.
But, my Elspie, he said, you would like to see, I fancy,
Something of the world, of men and women. You will
　　not refuse me,
You will one day come with me and see my uncle and
　　cousins,
Sister, and brother, and brother's wife. You should go,
　　if you liked it,
Just as you are; just what you are, at any rate, my Elspie.

Yes, we will go, and give the old solemn gentility stage-play
One little look, to leave it with all the more satisfaction.

That may be, my Philip, she said; you are good to
think of it.
But we are letting our fancies run on indeed; after all,
It may all come, you know, Mr. Philip, to nothing whatever,
There is so much that needs to be done, so much that
may happen.
All that needs to be done, said he, shall be done, and
quickly.

And on the morrow he took good heart, and spoke
with David.
Not unwarned the father, nor had been unperceiving:
Fearful much, but in all from the first reassured by Adam.
In the first few days after Philip came to the bothie,
They had become hearty friends, full of trust the one in
the other:
And, in these last three, he had talked with him much,
and tried him.
And he remembered how at the first he had liked the lad;
and
Then, too, the old man's eye was much more for inner
than outer,
And the natural tune of his heart without misgiving
Went to the noble words of that grand song of the
Lowlands,

*Rank is the guinea stamp, but the man's a man for a'
that.*

Still he was doubtful, would hear nothing of it now,
  but insisted
Philip should go to his books; if he chose he might
  write; if after
Chose to return, might come; he truly believed him
  honest.
But a year must elapse, and many things might happen.
Yet at the end he burst into tears, called Elspie, and
  blessed them:
Elspie, my bairn, he said, I thought not when at the
  doorway
Standing with you, and telling the young man to come
  and see us,
I did not think he would one day be asking me here to
  surrender
What is to me more than wealth in my Bothie of Toper-
  na-fuosich.

IX.

Arva, beata Petamus arva!

So on the morrow's morrow, with Term-time dread
    returning,
Philip returned to his books, and read and remained at
    Oxford,
All the Christmas and Easter remained and read at
    Oxford.

Great was wonder in College when postman showed
    to butler
Letters addressed to David Mackaye at Toper-na-fuosich,
Letter on letter, at least one a week, one every Sunday:

Great at that Highland post was wonder too and con-
    jecture,
When the postman showed letters to wife, and wife to
    the lasses,
And the lasses declared they couldn't be really to David;
Yes, they could see inside a paper with E. upon it.

Great was surmise in College at breakfast, wine, and
    supper,
Keen the conjecture and joke ; but Adam kept the secret,

Adam the secret kept, and Philip read like fury.
  This is a letter written by Philip at Christmas to Adam:
What I said at Balloch has truth in it; only distorted.
Plants are some for fruit, and some for flowering only;
Let there be deer in parks, as well as kine in paddocks,
Grecian buildings upon the earth as well as Gothic.

  There may be men, perhaps, whose vocation it is to be
    idle,
Idle, sumptuous even, luxurious, if it must be:
Only let each man seek to be that for which nature meant
    him.
Independent surely of pleasure, if not regardless,
Independent also of station, if not regardless:
Irrespective alike of station as of enjoyment,
Do his duty in that state of life to which God, not man,
    shall call him.
If you were meant to plough, Lord Marquis, out with
    you, and do it!
If you were meant to be idle, O beggar, behold, I will
    feed thee,
Take my purse; you have far better right to it, friend,
    than the Marquis.
If you were born to be a groom, and you seem, by your
    dress, to believe so,
Do it like a man, Sir George, for pay, in a livery
    stable;
Yes, you may so release that slip of a boy at the corner,
Fingering books at the window, misdoubting the eighth
    commandment.

What, a mere Dean, with those wits, that debt-and-
creditor headpiece ?
Go, my detective DD., take the place of Burns the
gauger.
Ah, fair Lady Maria, God meant you to live and be
lovely ;
Be so then, and I bless you. But ye, ye spurious ware,
who
Might be plain women, and can be by no possibility
better !
—Ye unhappy statuettes, ye miserable trinkets,
Poor alabaster chimney-piece ornaments under glass cases,
Come, in God's name, come down ! The very French
clock by you
Puts you to shame with ticking; the fire-irons deride you,
Break your glasses, ye can ! come down, ye are not really
plaster,
Come, in God's name, come down ! do anything, but be
something !

You, young girl, who have had such advantages,
learnt so quickly,
Can you not teach ? O yes, and she likes Sunday-school
extremely,
Only it's soon in the morning. Away ! if to teach be
your calling,
It's no play, but a business: off! go teach and be paid
for it.
Surely that fussy old dowager yonder was meant for the
counter ;   •

Oh, she is notable, very, and keeps her servants in order
Past admiration.   Indeed, and keeps to employ her talent
How many, pray? to what use?   Away, the hotel's her
  vocation.
Lady Sophia's so good to the sick, so firm and so gentle.
Is there a nobler sphere than of hospital nurse or matron?
Hast thou for cooking a turn, little Lady Clarissa? in
  with them,
In with your fingers! their beauty it spoils, but your own
  it enhances;
For it is beautiful only to do the thing we are meant for.
But they will marry, have husbands, and children, and
  guests, and households—
Are there then so many trades for a man, for women one
  only,
First to look out for a husband, and then to preside at
  his table?
Learning to dance, then dancing, then breeding, and
  entertaining?
Breeding and rearing of children at any rate the poor do
Easier, says the doctors, and better, with all their slaving.
How many, too, disappointed, not being this, can be
  nothing!
How many more are spoilt for wives by the means to
  become so,
Spoilt for wives and mothers, and everything else more-
  over!

  This was the answer that came from the Tutor, the
  grave man, Adam:

Have you ever, Philip, my boy, looked at it in this way?
When the armies are set in array, and the battle
  beginning,
Is it well that the soldier whose post is far to the left-
  ward
Say, I will go to the right, it is there I shall do best
  service?
There is a great Field Marshal, my friend, who arrays
  our battalions;
Let us to Providence trust, and abide and work in our
  stations.

This was the final retort from the eager impetuous
  Philip.
I am sorry to say your Providence puzzles me sadly;
Children of Circumstance are we to be? You answer,
  On no wise!
Where does circumstance end, and Providence, where
  begins it?
In the revolving sphere which is upper, which is under?
What are we to resist, and what are we to be friends
  with?
If there is battle, 'tis battle by night, I stand in the
  darkness,
Here in the mêlée of men, Ionian and Dorian on both
  sides,
Signal and password known: which is friend and which
  is foeman?
Is it a friend? I doubt, though he speak with the voice
  of a brother.

Still you are right, I suppose; you always are, and will
be :
Though I mistrust the Field Marshal, I bow to the duty
of order.
Let us all get on as we can, and do what we're meant
for,
Or, as is said in your favourite weary old Ethics, our
ergon.
Yet is my feeling rather to ask, Where *is* the battle ?
Yes, I could find in my heart to cry, in spite of my
Elspie,
O that the armies indeed were arrayed ! O joy of the
onset !
Sound, thou Trumpet of God, come forth, Great Cause,
to array us,
King and leader appear, thy soldiers sorrowing seek
thee ;
Would that the armies indeed were arrayed : O where is
the battle ?
Neither battle I see, nor arraying, nor King in Israel,
Only infinite jumble, and mess, and dislocation,
Backed by a solemn appeal, For God's sake, do not stir,
there !
Yet you are right, I suppose : if you don't attack my
conclusion,
Let us get on as we can, and hunt for and do the ergon.
That isn't likely to be by sitting still, eating, and
drinking.
Yes, you are right, I dare say, you always were and
will be,

And in default of a fight I will put up with peace and
Elspie.

These are fragments again without date addressed to
Adam :
As at return of tide the total weight of ocean,
Drawn by moon and sun from Labrador and Greenland,
Sets in amain, in the open space betwixt Mull and
Scarba,
Heaving, swelling, spreading the might of the mighty
Atlantic ;
There into cranny and slit of the rocky, cavernous
bottom
Settles down, and with dimples huge the smooth sea-
surface
Eddies, coils, and whirls, by dangerous Corryvreckan :
So in my soul of souls, through its cells and secret
recesses,
Comes back, swelling and spreading, the old democratic
fervour.

But as the light of day enters some populous city,
Shaming away, ere it come, by the chilly day-streak
signal,
High and low, the misusers of night, shaming out the
gas-lamps—
All the great empty streets are flooded with broadening
clearness,
Which, withal, by inscrutable simultaneous access
Permeates far and pierces to very cellars lying in
Narrow high back-lane, and court, and alley of alleys :—

He that goes forth to his walk, while speeding to the
   suburb,
Sees sights only peaceful and pure; as, labourers settling
Slowly to work, in their limbs the lingering sweetness of
   slumber;
Humble market-carts, coming in, bringing in, not only
Flower, fruit, farm-store, but sounds and sights of the
   country,
Dwelling yet on the sense of the dreamy drivers: soon
   after
Half-awake servant-maids unfastening drowsy shutters
Up at the windows, or down, letting in the air by the
   doorway;
Schoolboys, schoolgirls soon, with slate, portfolio,
   satchel,
Hampered as they haste, those running, these others
   maidenly tripping;
Early clerk anon turning out to stroll, or it may be
Meet his sweetheart, waiting behind the garden-gate
   there;
Merchant on his grass-plat haply, bare-headed; and now
   by this time
Little child bringing breakfast to "father" that sits on
   the timber,
There by the scaffolding; see, she waits for the can
   beside him;
Meantime, above, purer air, untarnished of new-lit fires:
So that the whole great wicked artificial civilised fabric,—
All its unfinished houses, lots for sale, and railway out-
   works,—

Seems re-accepted, resumed to primal nature and
  beauty :—
—Such, in me, and to me, and on me, the love of
  Elspie !

Philip returned to his books, but returned to his High-
  lands after ;
Got a "first," 'tis said ; a winsome bride, 'tis certain.
There while courtship was ending, nor yet the wedding
  appointed,
Under her father he learnt to handle the hoe and the
  hatchet :
Thither that summer succeeding came Adam and Arthur
  to see him,
Down by the lochs from the distant Glenmorison : Adam
  the Tutor,
Arthur, and Hope ; and the Piper anon, who was there
  for a visit.
He had been into the "Schools"; plucked almost ;
  almost a *gone-coon*,
So he declared; never once had brushed up his *hairy*
  Aldrich;
Into the great might-have-been upsoaring, sublime and
  ideal,
Gave to historical questions a free poetical treatment ;
Leaving vocabular ghosts undisturbed in their lexicon-
  limbo,
Took Aristophanes up at a shot ; and the whole three
  last weeks

Went in his life and the sunshine rejoicing to Nuneham
and Godstowe.
What were the claims of Degree to those of life and the
sunshine?
—There did the four find Philip, the poet, the speaker,
the Chartist,
Delving at Highland soil, and railing at Highland land-
lords,
Railing, but more, as it seemed, for the fun of the Piper's
fury.
There saw they David and Elspie Mackaye, and the
Piper was almost,
Almost deeply in love with Bella the sister of Elspie;
But the good Adam was heedful; they did not go too
often.
There in the bright October, the gorgeous bright October,
When the brackens are changed, and heather blooms are
faded,
And amid russet of heather and fern green trees are
bonnie,
There, when shearing had ended, and barley-stooks
were garnered,
David gave Philip to wife his daughter, his darling
Elspie;
Elspie the quiet, the brave, was wedded to Philip the
poet.

So won Philip his bride. They are married and gone
—But oh, thou

Mighty one, Muse of great Epos, and Idyll the playful
   and tender,
Be it recounted in song, ere we part, and thou fly to thy
   Pindus,
(Pindus is it, O Muse, or Aetna, or even Ben Nevis?)
Be it recounted in song, O Muse of the Epos and Idyll,
Who gave what at the wedding, the gifts and fair gratu-
   lations.

Adam, the grave careful Adam, a medicine-chest and
   tool-box,
Hope a saddle, and Arthur a plough, and a rifle the
   Piper,
Airlie a necklace for Elspie, and Hobbes a Family
   Bible,
Airlie a necklace, and Hobbes a Bible and iron bedstead.

What was the letter, O Muse, sent withal by the
   corpulent hero?
This is the letter of Hobbes, the kilted and corpulent
   hero.

So the last speech and confession is made, O my
   eloquent speaker!
So *the good time* is *coming*,—or come, is it?　O my
   Chartist!
So the cathedral is finished at last, O my Pugin of
   Women;
Finished, and now—is it true?—to be taken out whole
   to New Zealand!

Well, go forth to thy field, to thy barley, with Ruth, O
    Boaz,
Ruth who for thee hath deserted her people, her gods,
    her mountains,
Quitted her Moab-Lochaber for thee, thou Naomi-Boaz.
Go, as in Ephrath of old, in the gates of Bethlehem said
    they,
Go, be the wife in thy house both Rachel and Leah unto
    thee !
Be thy wedding of silver, albeit of iron thy bedstead !
Yea, to the full golden fifty be lengthened ! while fair
    memoranda
Duly fill up the fly-leaves duly left in the Family
    Bible.
Live, be happy, and look too to keep a whole skin on
    thy sirloin.
Live, and when Hobbes is forgotten, may'st thou, an
    unroasted Grandsire,
See thy children's children, and Democracy upon New
    Zealand !

This was the letter of Hobbes, and this is the postscript
    after.
Wit in the letter will prate, but wisdom speaks in a
    postscript ;
Listen to wisdom—*Which things*—you perhaps didn't
    know, my dear fellow,
I have reflected: *Which things are an allegory*, Philip.
For this Rachel-and-Leah is marriage ; which, I have
    seen it,

Lo, and have known it, is always, and must be, bigamy
only,
Even in noblest kind a duality, compound and complex,
One part heavenly-ideal, the other vulgar and earthy :
For this Rachel-and-Leah is marriage, and Laban their
father
Circumstance, chance, the world, our uncle and hard
task-master.
Rachel we found as we fled from the daughters of Heth
by the desert ;
Rachel we met at the well ; we came, we saw, we kissed
her ;
Rachel we serve for, long years, that seem a few days
only,
E'en for the love we have to her, and win her at last of
Laban.
Is it not Rachel we take in our joy from the hand of her
father ?
Is it not Rachel we lead in the mystical veil from the
altar ?
Rachel we dream of at night : in the morning, behold, it
is Leah.

Nay, it is custom, saith Laban, and Leah indeed is the
elder :
Happy and wise who consents to redouble his service to
Laban,
So, fulfilling her week, he may add to the elder the
younger,
Not repudiates Leah, but wins him the Rachel unto her !

Neither hate thou thy Leah, my Philip, she also is
    worthy ;
So, many days shall thy Rachel have joy, and survive her
    sister :
Yea and her children.— *Which things are an allegory*,
    Philip,
Aye, and, by Origen's head, with a vengeance too, a
    long one !

This was a note from the Tutor, the grave man, nick-
    named Adam.
I shall see you, of course, my Philip, before your de-
    parture ;
Joy be with you, my boy, with you and your beautiful
    Elspie.
Happy is he that found, and finding was not heedless;
Happy is he that found, and happy the friend that was
    with him.
    So won Philip his bride :—

They are married and gone to New Zealand,
Five hundred pounds in pocket, with books, and two or
    three pictures,
Tool-box, plough, and the rest, they rounded the sphere
    to New Zealand.
There he hewed, and dug ; subdued the earth and his
    spirit ;
There he built him a home ; there Elspie bare him his
    children,

David and Bella; perhaps ere this too an Elspie or
    Adam.
There hath he farmstead and land, and fields of corn and
    flax fields;
And the Antipodes too have a Bothie of Toper-na-fuosich.

POEMS FROM "AMBARVALIA."

.

Poems from "Ambarvalia."

"THE HUMAN SPIRITS."

THE human spirits saw I on a day,
Sitting and looking each a different way;
And hardly tasking, subtly questioning,
Another spirit went around the ring
To each and each : and as he ceased his say,
Each after each, I heard them singly sing,
Some querulously high, some softly, sadly low,
We know not,—what avails to know?
We know not,—wherefore need we know?
This answer gave they still unto his suing,
We know not, let us do as we are doing.

Dost thou not know that these things only seem ?-
I know not, let me dream my dream.
Are dust and ashes fit to make a treasure?—
I know not, let me take my pleasure.
What shall avail the knowledge thou hast sought?—
I know not, let me think my thought.

What is the end of strife?—
I know not, let me live my life.
How many days or e'er thou mean'st to move?—
I know not, let me love my love.
Were not things old once new?—
I know not, let me do as others do.
And when the rest were over past,
I know not, I will do my duty, said the last.

Thy duty do? rejoined the voice,
Ah do it, do it, and rejoice;
But shalt thou then, when all is done,
Enjoy a love, embrace a beauty
Like these, that may be seen and won
In life, whose course will then be run;—
Or wilt thou be where there is none?—
I know not, I will do my duty.

And taking up the word around, above, below,
Some querulously high, some softly, sadly low,
We know not, sang they, nor ever need we know!
We know not, sang they, what avails to know?
Whereat the questioning spirit, some short space,
Though unabashed, stood quiet in his place.
But as the echoing chorus died away
And to their dreams the rest returned apace,
By the one spirit I saw him kneeling low,
And in a silvery whisper heard him say:

Truly, thou know'st not, and thou need'st not know;
Hope only, hope thou, and believe alway ;
I also know not, and I need not know,
Only with questioning pass I to and fro,
Perplexing these that sleep, and in their folly
Imbreeding doubt and sceptic melancholy ;
Till that their dreams deserting, they with me
Come all to this true ignorance and thee.

THE POET'S LOVE.

I.

Ah, what is love, our love, she said,
  Ah, what is human love?
A fire, of earthly fuel fed,
  Full fain to soar above.
With lambent flame the void it lips,
  And of the impassive air
Would frame for its ambitious steps
  A heaven-attaining stair.
It wrestles and it climbs—Ah me,
  Go look in little space,
White ash on blackened earth will be
  Sole record of its place.

II.

Ah love, high love, she said and sighed,
  She said, the Poet's love !
A star upon a turbid tide,
  Reflected from above.
A marvel here, a glory there,
  But clouds will intervene,
And garish earthly noon outglare
  The purity serene.

"I GIVE THEE JOY."

I GIVE thee joy ! O worthy word !
Congratulate.—A courtier fine
Transacts, politely shuffling by,
The civil ceremonial lie,
Which, quickly spoken, barely heard,
Can never hope, nor e'en design
　　　　　To give thee joy !

I give thee joy ! O faithful word !
When heart with heart, and mind with mind
Shake hands; and eyes in outward sign
Of inward vision, rest in thine ;
And feelings simply, truly stirred,
Emphatic utterance seek to find,
　　　　　And give thee joy !

I give thee joy ! O word of power !
Believe, though slight the lie in sooth,
When heart to heart its fountain opes
The plant to water that with hopes
Is budding for fruition's flower—
The word, potential made, in truth
　　　　　Shall give thee joy !

Shall give thee joy! Oh, not in vain
For erring child the mother's prayer;
The sigh, wherein a martyr's breath
Exhales from ignominious death
For some lost cause! In humbler strain
Shall this poor word a virtue bear,
     And give thee joy!

"WHEN PANTING SIGHS THE BOSOM FILL."

WHEN panting sighs the bosom fill,
And hands by chance united thrill
At once with one delicious pain
The pulses and the nerves of twain;
When eyes, that erst could meet with ease,
Do seek, yet, seeking, slyly shun
Ecstatic conscious unison,—
The sure beginnings, say, be these,
Prelusive to the strain of love
Which angels sing in heaven above?

Or is it but the vulgar tune,
Which all that breathe beneath the moon
So accurately learn—so soon?
With variations duly blent,
Yet that same song to all intent
Set for the finer instrument;
It is: and it would sound the same
In beasts, were not the bestial frame,
Less subtly organised, to blame;
And but that soul and spirit add
To pleasures, even base and bad,
A zest the soulless never had.

It may be—well indeed I deem;
But what if sympathy, it seem,

And admiration and esteem,
Commingling therewithal, do make
The passion prized for Reason's sake?
Yet, when my heart would fain rejoice
A small expostulating voice
Falls in : Of this thou wilt not take
Thy one irrevocable choice?
In accent tremulous and thin
I hear high Prudence deep within,
Pleading the bitter, bitter sting,
Should slow-maturing seasons bring,
Too late, the veritable thing.
For if (the Poet's tale of bliss)
A love, wherewith commeasured, this
Is weak, and beggarly, and none,—
Exist, a treasure to be won,
And if the vision, though it stay,
Be yet for an appointed day,—
This choice, if made, this deed, if done,
The memory of this present past,
With vague foreboding might o'ercast
The heart, or madden it at last.

Let Reason first her office ply ;
Esteem, and admiration high,
And mental, moral sympathy,
Exist they first, nor be they brought
By self-deceiving afterthought,—
What if a halo interfuse

With these again its opal hues,
That all o'erspreading and o'erlying,
Transmuting, mingling, glorifying,
About the beauteous various whole,
With beaming smile do dance and quiver;
Yet, is that halo of the soul?—
Or is it, as may sure be said,
Phosphoric exhalation bred
Of vapour steaming from the bed
Of Fancy's brook, or Passion's river?
So when, as will be by-and-by,
The stream is waterless and dry,
This halo and its hues will die:
And though the soul contented rest
With those substantial blessings blest,
Will not a longing, half-confessed,
Betray that this is not the love,
The gift for which, all gifts above,
Him praise we Who is Love, the giver?

I cannot say—the things are good:
Bread is it, if not angels' food;
But Love? Alas! I cannot say;
A glory on the vision lay;
A light of more than mortal day
About it played, upon it rested;
It did not, faltering and weak,
Beg Reason on its side to speak,
Itself was Reason, or, if not,

Such substitute as is, I wot,
Of seraph-kind the loftier lot;—
Itself was of itself attested ;
To processes that, hard and dry,
Elaborate truth from fallacy,
With modes intuitive succeeding,
Including these and superseding ;
Reason sublimed and Love most high
It was, a life that cannot die,
A dream of glory most exceeding.

AS, AT A RAILWAY JUNCTION.

As, at a railway junction, men
Who came together, taking then
One the train up, one down, again

Meet never ! Ah, much more as they
Who take one street's two sides, and say
Hard parting words, but walk one way :

Though moving other mates between,
While carts and coaches intervene,
Each to the other goes unseen,

Yet seldom, surely shall there lack
Knowledge they walk not back to back,
But with an unity of track,

Where common dangers each attend,
And common hopes their guidance lend
To light them to the self-same end.

Whether he then shall cross to thee,
Or thou go thither, or it be
Some midway point, ye yet shall see

Each other, yet again shall meet,
Ah, joy ! when with the closing street,
Forgivingly at last ye greet !

COMMEMORATION SONNETS.

OXFORD, 1844.

I.

AMIDST the fleeting many unforgot,
O Leonina ! whether thou wert seen
Singling, upon the Isis' margent green,
From meaner flowers the frail forget-me-not,
Or, as the picture of a saintly queen,
Sitting, uplifting, betwixt fingers small,
A sceptre of the water-iris tall,
With pendent lily crowned of golden sheen;
So, or in gay and gorgeous gallery,
When, amid splendours, like to those that far
Flame backward from the sun's invisible ear,
Thou lookedst forth, as then the evening star ;
O Leonina ! fair wert thou to see,
And unforgotten shall thine image be.

II.

Thou whom thy danglers have ere this forgot,
O Leonina ! whether thou wert seen
Waiting, upon the Isis' margent green,
The boats that should have passed there, and did not ;
Or at the ball, admiring crowds between,
To partner academical and slow

Teaching, upon the light Slavonic toe,
Polkas that were not, only should have been;
Or in the crowded gallery crushed, didst hear
For bonnets white, blue, pink, the ladies' cheer
Multiplied while divided, and endure
(Myself being seen) to see, not hear, rehearse
The long, long Proses, and the Latin Verse—
O Leonina! thou wert tired, I'm sure.

III.

Not in thy robes of royal rich array,
As when thy state at Dresden thou art keeping;
Nor with the golden epaulettes outpeeping
From under pink and scarlet trappings gay
(Raiment of doctors) through the area led;
While galleries peal applause, and Phillimore
For the supreme superlative cons o'er
The commonplace-book of his classic head;
Uncrown'd thou com'st, alone, or with a tribe
Of volant varlets scattering jest and jibe
Almost beside thee.   Yet to thee, when rent
Was the Teutonic Cæsar's robe, there went
One portion : and with Julius, thou to-day
Canst boast, I came, I saw, I went away!

COME BACK AGAIN, MY OLDEN HEART!

Come back again, my olden heart !—
  Ah, fickle spirit and untrue,
I bade the only guide depart
  Whose faithfulness I surely knew:
I said, My heart is all too soft ;
He who would climb and soar aloft,
Must needs keep ever at his side
The tonic of a wholesome pride.

Come back again, my olden heart !—
  Alas, I called not then for thee ;
I called for courage, and apart
  From pride if·courage could not be,
Then welcome, pride ! and I shall find
In thee a power to lift the mind
This low and grovelling joy above—
'Tis but the proud can truly love.

Come back again, my olden heart !—
  With incrustations of the years
Uncased as yet,—as then thou wert,
  Fulfilled with shame and coward fears :
Wherewith, amidst a jostling throng
Of deeds, that each and all were wrong,
The doubting soul, from day to day,
Uneasy, paralytic lay.

Come back again, my olden heart !—
   I said, Perceptions contradict,
Convictions come, anon depart.
   And but themselves as false convict.
Assumptions hasty, crude, and vain,
Full oft to use will science deign ;
The corks the novice plies to-day
The swimmer soon shall cast away.

Come back again, my olden heart !—
   I said, Behold, I perish quite,
Unless to give me strength to start,
   I make myself my rule of right :
It must be, if I act at all,
To save my shame I have at call
The plea of all men understood,—
' Because I willed it, it is good.'

Come back again, my olden heart !—
   I know not if in very deed
This means alone could aid impart
   To serve my sickly spirit's need ;
But clear alike of wild self-will,
And fear that faltered, paltered still,
Remorseful thoughts of after days
A way espy betwixt the ways.

Come back again, old heart ! Ah, me !
   Methinks in those thy coward fears

There might, perchance, a courage be,
　That fails in these the manlier years;
Courage to let the courage sink,
Itself a coward base to think,
Rather than not for heavenly light
Wait on to show the truly right.

"WHEN SOFT SEPTEMBER BRINGS AGAIN."

When soft September brings again
  To yonder gorse its golden glow,
And Snowdon sends its autumn rain
  To bid thy current livelier flow ;
Amid that ashen foliage light
When scarlet beads are glistering bright,
While alder-boughs unchanged are seen
In summer livery of green ;
When clouds before the cooler breeze
Are flying, white and large ; with these
Returning, so may I return,
And find thee changeless, Pont-y-wern.

"OH, ASK NOT WHAT IS LOVE, SHE SAID."

OH, ask not what is love, she said,
   Or ask it not of me;
Or of the heart, or of the head,
   Or if at all it be.

Oh, ask it not, she said, she said,
   Thou winn'st not word from me!
Oh, silent as the long long dead,
   I, lady, learn of thee.

I ask,—thou speakest not,—and still
   I ask, and look to thee;
And lo, without or with a will,
   The answer is in me.

Without thy will it came to me?
   Ah, with it let it stay;
Ah, with it, yes, abide in me,
   Not only for to-day!

Thou claim'st it? nay, the deed is done;
   Ah, leave it with thy leave;
And then a thousand loves for one
   Shalt day on day receive.

A WOMAN'S PROTEST.

LIGHT words they were, and lightly, falsely said ;
She heard them, and she started,—and she rose,
As in the act to speak; the sudden thought
And unconsidered impulse led her on.
In act to speak she rose, but with the sense
Of all the eyes of that mixed company
Now suddenly turned upon her, some with age
Hardened and dulled, some cold and critical ;
Some in whom vapours of their own conceit,
As most malarious mists the heavenly stars,
Still blotted out their good, the best at best
By frivolous laugh and prate conventional
All too untuned for all she thought to say—
With such a thought the mantling blood to her cheek
Flushed up, and o'erflushed itself; blank night her soul
Made dark, and in her all her purpose swooned.
She stood as if for sinking.   Yet anon
With recollections clear, august, sublime,
Of God's great truth, and right immutable,
Which, as obedient vassals, to her mind
Came summoned of her will, in self-negation
Quelling her troublous earthy consciousness,
She queened it o'er her weakness.   At the spell
Back rolled the ruddy tide, and leaves her cheek
Paler than erst, and yet not ebbs so far
But that one pulse of one indignant thought
Might hurry it hither in flood.   So as she stood
She spoke.   God in her spoke, and made her heard.

QUI LABORAT, ORAT.

O ONLY Source of all our light and life,
  Whom as our truth, our strength, we see and feel,
But whom the hours of mortal moral strife,
  Alone aright reveal,—

Mine inmost soul, before Thee inly brought,
  Thy presence owns, ineffable, divine ;
Chastised each rebel self-encentred thought,
  My will adoreth Thine.

With eye down-dropt, if then this earthly mind
  Speechless abide, or speechless e'en depart ;
Nor seek to see—for what of earthly kind
  Can see Thee as Thou art ?—

If sure-assured 'tis but profanely bold
  In thought's abstractest forms to seem to see,
It dare not dare the dread communion hold
  In ways unworthy Thee,

O not unowned, Thou shalt, unnamed, forgive ;
  In worldly walks the prayerless heart prepare ;
And if in work its life it seem to live,
  Shall make that work be prayer.

Nor times shall lack, when, while the work it plies,
  Unsummoned powers the blinding film shall part,
And, scarce by happy tears made dim, the eyes
  In recognition start.

As wills Thy will, or give, or e'en forbear
  The beatific supersensual sight,
So, with Thy blessing blest, that humbler prayer
  Approach Thee morn and night.

"WITH GRACEFUL SEAT AND SKILFUL HAND."

WITH graceful seat and skilful hand,
  Upon the fiery steed,
Prompt at a moment to command,
  As fittest, or concede.

O Lady ! happy he whose will
  Shall manliest homage pay
To that which yielding ever, still
  Shall in its yielding sway :

Yea, happy he, whose willing soul
  In perfect love combined
With mine shall form one perfect whole,
  One happy heart and mind !

Fair, fair in fleeting steed to see,
  Boon nature's child, nor less,
In gorgeous rooms, serene and free,
  Midst etiquette and dress !

Thrice happy who, amidst the form
  And folly that must be,
Existence fresh, and true, and warm,
  Shall, Lady, own in thee !

Such dreams, in gay saloon, of days
  That shall be, 'midst the dance
And music, while I hear and gaze,
  My silent soul entrance.

As here the harp thy fingers wake
  No sounds melodious, he
To thy soul's touch shall music make,
  And his enstrengthen thee.

The notes, diverse in time and tone,
  The hearts shall image true,
That still, in some sweet ways unknown,
  Their harmonies renew.

The mazy dance, an emblem meet,
  Shall changeful life portray,
Whose changes all love's music sweet
  Expressively obey.

Then shall to waltz, though unexiled,
  And polka sometimes heard,
To songs, capricious, wayward, wild,
  Be other strains preferred.

The heart that midst the petty strife,
  Whose ferment, day by day,
To strange realities of life
  Converts its trifling play,—

The heart that here pursued the right,
  Shall then, in freer air,
Expand its wings, and drink the light
  Of life and reason there:

And quickening truth and living law,
  And large affections clear,
Shall it to heights on heights updraw,
  To holiest hope and fear.

—Ah, moralising premature!
  And yet words half-supprest
May find some secret thoughts ensure
  Acceptance half-confest.

Full oft concealed high meanings work;
  And, scorning observation,
In gay unthinking guise will lurk
  A saintly aspiration;

No sickly thing to sit and sun
  Its puny worth, to pause
And list, ere half the deed be done,
  Its echo—self-applause.

No idler, who its kindly cares
  To every gossip mentions,
And at its breast a posy wears
  Of laudable inventions.

As of itself, of others so
 Unrecognised, to seek
Its aim content, and in the flow
 Of life and spirits meek.

WHEN ISRAEL CAME OUT OF EGYPT.

Lo, here is God, and there is God !
   Believe it not, O man ;
In such vain sort to this and that
   The ancient heathen ran :
Though old Religion shake her head,
   And say in bitter grief,
" The day behold, at first foretold,
   Of atheist unbelief" :
Take better part, with manly heart,
   Thine adult spirit can ;
Receive it not, believe it not,
   Believe it not, O man !

As men at dead of night awaked
   With cries, " The King is here,"
Rush forth and greet whome'er they meet,
   Whoe'er shall first appear ;
And still repeat, to all the street,
   " 'Tis he,—the King is here ; "
The long procession moveth on,
   Each nobler form they see
With changeful suit they still salute,
   And cry, " 'Tis he, 'tis he ! "

So, even so, when men were young,
   And earth and heaven was new,

WHEN ISRAEL CAME.

And His immediate presence He
  From human hearts withdrew,
The soul perplexed and daily vexed
  With sensuous False and True,
Amazed, bereaved, no less believed,
  And fain would see Him too :
" He is ! " the prophet-tongues proclaimed ;
  In joy and hasty fear,
" He is ! " aloud replied the crowd, —
  " Is here, and here, and here."

" He is ! They are ! in distance seen
  On yon Olympus high,
In those Avernian woods abide,
  And walk this azure sky :
" They are, they are ! " to every show
  Its eyes the baby turned,
And blazes sacrificial tall
  On thousand altars burned :
" They are, they are ! "—On Sinai's top
  Far seen the lightnings shone,
The thunder broke, a trumpet spoke,
  And God said, I am One.

God spake it out, I, God, am One ;
  The unheeding ages ran,
And baby-thoughts again, again,
  Have dogged the growing man :

And as of old from Sinai's top
    God said that God is One,
By Science strict so speaks He now
    To tell us, There is None !
Earth goes by chemic forces ; Heaven's
    A Mécanique Celeste !
And heart and mind of human kind
    A watch-work as the rest !

Is this a Voice, as was the Voice
    Whose speaking spoke abroad,
When thunder pealed, and mountain reeled,
    The ancient Truth of God?
Ah, not the voice; 'tis but the cloud,
    The cloud of darkness dense,
Where image none, nor e'er was seen
    Similitude of sense.
'Tis but the cloudy darkness dense
    That wrapt the Mount around ;
With dull amaze the people stays,
    And doubts the Coming Sound.

Some chosen prophet-soul the while
    Shall dare, sublimely meek,
Within the shroud of blackest cloud
    The Deity to seek :
'Midst atheistic systems dark,
    And darker hearts' despair,

That soul has heard His very word,
  And on the dusky air
His skirts, as passed He by, to see
  Has strained on their behalf,
Who on the plain, with dance amain,
  Adore the Golden Calf.

'Tis but the cloudy darkness dense ;
  Though blank the tale it tells,
No God, no Truth ! yet He, in sooth,
  Is there—within it dwells ;
Within the sceptic darkness deep
  He dwells that none may see,
Till idol-forms and idol-thoughts
  Have passed and ceased to be :
No God, no Truth ! ah, though, in sooth,
  So stands the doctrine's half,
On Egypt's track return not back,
  Nor own the Golden Calf.

Take better part, with manlier heart,
  Thine adult spirit can ;
No God, no Truth,—receive it ne'er—
  Believe it ne'er—O Man !
But turn not then to seek again
  What first the ill began ;

No God, it saith ; ah, wait in faith
  God's self-completing plan ;
Receive it not, but leave it not,
  And wait it out, O Man !

The Man that went the cloud within
  Is gone and vanished quite ;
He cometh not, the people cries,
  Nor bringeth God to sight :
Lo these thy gods that safety give,
  Adore and keep the feast !—
Deluding and deluded cries
  The Prophet's brother-priest :
And Israel all bows down to fall
  Before the gilded beast.

Devout indeed ! that priestly creed,
  O Man, reject as sin ;
The clouded hill attend thou still,
  And him that went within.
He yet shall bring some worthy thing
  For waiting souls to see ;
Some sacred word that he hath heard
  Their light and life shall be ;
Some lofty part, than which the heart
  Adopt no nobler can,
Thou shalt receive, thou shalt believe,
  And thou shalt do, O Man !

THE SILVER WEDDING.

THE Silver Wedding ! on some pensive ear
From towers remote as sound the silvery bells,
To-day from one far unforgotten year
A silvery faint memorial music swells.

And silver-pale the dim memorial light
Of musing age on youthful joys is shed,
The golden joys of fancy's dawning bright,
The golden bliss of, Woo'd, and won, and wed.

Ah, golden then, but silver now ! In sooth,
The years that pale the cheek, that dim the eyes,
And silver o'er the golden hairs of youth,
Less prized can make its only priceless prize.

Not so ; the voice this silver name that gave
To this, the ripe and unenfeebled date,
For steps together tottering to the grave,
Hath bid the perfect golden title wait.

Rather, if silver this, if that be gold,
From good to better changed on age's track,
Must it as baser metal be enrolled,
That day of days, a quarter-century back.

Yet ah, its hopes, its joys were golden too,
　But golden of the fairy gold of dreams :
To feel is but to dream ; until we do,
　There's nought that is, and all we see but seems.

What was or seemed it needed cares and tears,
　And deeds together done, and trials past,
And all the subtlest alchemy of years,
　To change to genuine substance here at last.

Your fairy gold is silver sure to-day ;
　Your ore by crosses many, many a loss,
As in refiners' fires, hath purged away
　What erst it had of earthy human dross.

Come years as many yet, and as they go,
　In human life's great crucible shall they
Transmute, so potent are the spells they know,
　Into pure gold the silver of to-day.

Strange metallurge is human life ! 'Tis true ;
　And Use and Wont in many a gorgeous case
Full specious fair for casual outward view
　Electrotype the sordid and the base.

Nor lack who praise, avowed, the spurious ware,
　Who bid young hearts the one true love forego,
Conceit to feed, or fancy light as air,
　Or greed of pelf and precedence and show.

True, false, as one to casual eyes appear,
  To read men truly men may hardly learn;
Yet doubt it not that wariest glance would here
  Faith, Hope and Love, the true Tower-stamp discern.

Come years again! as many yet ! and purge
  Less precious earthier elements away,
And gently changed at life's extremest verge,
  Bring bright in gold your perfect fiftieth day !

That sight may children see and parents show !
  If not—yet earthly chains of metal true,
By love and duty wrought and fixed below,
  Elsewhere will shine, transformed, celestial-new ;

Will shine of gold, whose essence, heavenly bright,
  No doubt-damps tarnish, worldly passions fray ;
Gold into gold there mirrored, light in light,
  Shall gleam in glories of a deathless day.

THE TWO MUSICS.

I.

WHY should I say I see the things I see not?
  Why be and be not?
Show love for that I love not, and fear for what I fear not?
And dance about to music that I hear not?
    Who standeth still i' the street
    Shall be hustled and justled about;
And he that stops i' the dance shall be spurned by the
    dancers' feet,—
Shall be shoved and be twisted by all he shall meet,
    And shall raise up an outcry and rout;
      And the partner, too,—
      What's the partner to do?
While all the while 'tis but, perchance, an humming in
    mine ear,
    That yet anon shall hear,
    And I anon, the music in my soul,
    In a moment read the whole;
    The music in my heart,
    Joyously take my part,
And hand in hand, and heart with heart, with these
    retreat, advance;
    And borne on wings of wavy sound,
    Whirl with these around, around,
  Who here are living in the living dance!
    Why forfeit that fair chance?

Till that arrive, till thou awake,
Of these, my soul, thy music make,
And keep amid the throng,
And turn as they shall turn, and bound as they are
        bounding,—
Alas! alas! alas! and what if all along
The music is not sounding?

II.

Are there not, then, two musics unto men?—
        One loud and bold and coarse,
        And overpowering still perforce
        All tone and tune beside;
        Yet in despite its pride
Only of fumes of foolish fancy bred,
And sounding solely in the sounding head:
        The other, soft and low,
        Stealing whence we not know,
Painfully heard, and easily forgot,
With pauses oft and many a silence strange
(And silent oft it seems, when silent it is not),
Revivals too of unexpected change:
Haply thou think'st 'twill never be begun,
Or that 't has come, and been, and passed away:
        Yet turn to other none,—
        Turn not, oh, turn not thou!
But listen, listen, listen,—if haply be heard it may;
Listen, listen, listen,—is it not sounding now?

III.

Yea, and as thought of some beloved friend
By death or distance parted will descend,
Severing, in crowded rooms ablaze with light,
As by a magic screen, the seër from the sight
(Palsying the nerves that intervene
The eye and central sense between);
    So may the ear,
    Hearing not hear,
Though drums do roll, and pipes and cymbals ring;
So the bare conscience of the better thing
Unfelt, unseen, unimaged, all unknown,
May fix the entrancèd soul 'mid multitudes alone.

"SWEET STREAMLET BASON."

SWEET streamlet bason! at thy side
Weary and faint within me cried
My longing heart;—In such pure deep
How sweet it were to sit and sleep!
To feel each passage from without
Close up,—above me and about,
Those circling waters crystal clear,
That calm impervious atmosphere!
There on thy pearly pavement pure,
To lean, and feel myself secure,
Or through the dim-lit inter-space,
Afar at whiles upgazing trace
The dimpling bubbles dance around
Upon thy smooth exterior face;
Or idly list the dreamy sound
Of ripples lightly flung, above
That home, of peace, if not of love?

VAIN PHILOSOPHY.

Away, haunt not thou me,
Thou vain Philosophy !
Little hast thou bestead,
Save to perplex the head,
And leave the spirit dead.
Unto thy broken cisterns wherefore go,
While from the secret treasure-depths below,
Fed by the skyey shower,
And clouds that sink and rest on hill-tops high,
Wisdom at once, and Power,
Are welling, bubbling forth, unseen, incessantly?
Why labour at the dull mechanic oar,
When the fresh breeze is blowing,
And the strong current flowing,
Right onward to the Eternal Shore?

"MY WIND IS TURNED TO BITTER NORTH."

My wind is turned to bitter north,
 That was so soft a south before;
My sky, that shone so sunny bright,
 With foggy gloom is clouded o'er:
My gay green leaves are yellow-black,
 Upon the dank autumnal floor;
For love, departed once, comes back
 No more again, no more.

A roofless ruin lies my home,
 For winds to blow and rains to pour;
One frosty night befell, and lo!
 I find my summer days are o'er:
The heart bereaved, of why and how
 Unknowing, knows that yet before
It had what e'en to Memory now
 Returns no more, no more.

"THOUGHT MAY WELL BE EVER RANGING."

THOUGHT may well be ever ranging,
And opinion ever changing,
Task-work be, though ill begun,
Dealt with by experience better,
By the law and by the letter
Duty done is duty done :
Do it, Time is on the wing !

Hearts, 'tis quite another thing,
Must or once for all be given,
Or must not at all be given ;
Hearts, 'tis quite another thing !

To bestow the soul away
In an idle duty-play !—
Why, to trust a life-long bliss
To caprices of a day,
Scarce were more depraved than this !

Men and maidens, see you mind it ;
Show of love, where'er you find it,
Look if duty lurk behind it !
Duty-fancies, urging on
Whither love had never gone !

Loving—if the answering breast
Seem not to be thus possessed,
Still in hoping have a care;
If it do, beware, beware!
But if in yourself you find it,
Above all things—mind it, mind it!

DUTY.

Duty—that's to say complying
  With whate'er's expected here ;
On your unknown cousin's dying,
  Straight be ready with the tear :
Upon etiquette relying,
Unto usage nought denying,
Lend your waist to be embraced,
  Blush not even, never fear;
Claims of kith and kin connection,
  Claims of manners honour still,
Ready money of affection
  Pay, whoever drew the bill.
With the form conforming duly,
Senseless what it meaneth truly,
Go to church—the world require you,
  To balls, the world require you too,
And marry—papa and mamma desire you,
  And your sisters and schoolfellows do.
Duty—'tis to take on trust
What things are good, and right, and just ;
And whether indeed they be or be not,
Try not, test not, feel not, see not :
'Tis walk and dance, sit down and rise
By leading, opening ne'er your eyes ;
Stunt sturdy limbs that Nature gave,
And be drawn in a Bath-chair along to the grave.

'Tis the stern and prompt suppressing,
   As an obvious deadly sin,
All the questing and the guessing
   Of the soul's own soul within :
'Tis the coward acquiescence
   In a destiny's behest,
To a shade by terror made,
Sacrificing aye the essence
   Of all that's truest, noblest, best :
'Tis the blind non-recognition
   Either of goodness, truth or beauty,
Except by precept and submission ;
   Moral blank, and moral void,
   Life at very birth destroyed,
Atrophy, exinanition !
Duty!————
Yea, by duty's prime condition
   Pure nonentity of duty !

"BLANK MISGIVINGS OF A CREATURE
MOVING ABOUT IN WORLDS NOT REALISED."

I.

HERE am I yet, another twelvemonth spent,
One-third departed of the mortal span,
Carrying on the child into the man,
Nothing into reality.   Sails rent,
And rudder broken,—reason impotent,—
Affections all unfixed ; so forth I fare
On the mid seas unheedingly, so dare
To do and to be done by, well content.
So was it from the first, so is it yet ;
Yea, the first kiss that by these lips was set
On any human lips, methinks was sin—
Sin, cowardice, and falsehood ; for the will
Into a deed e'en then advanced, wherein
God, unidentified, was thought of still.

II.

Though to the vilest things beneath the moon
For poor ease' sake I give away my heart,
And for the moment's sympathy let part
My sight and sense of truth, Thy precious boon,
My painful earnings, lost, all lost, as soon,
Almost, as gained : and though aside I start,
Belie Thee daily, hourly,—still Thou art,

Art surely as in heaven the sun at noon :
How much so'er I sin, whate'er I do
Of evil, still the sky above is blue,
The stars look down in beauty as before :
Is it enough to walk as best we may,
To walk, and sighing, dream of that blest day
When ill we cannot quell shall be no more ?

III.

Well, well,—Heaven bless you all from day to day !
Forgiveness too, or e'er we part, from each,
As I do give it, so must I beseech :
I owe all much, much more than I can pay ;
Therefore it is I go ; how could I stay
When every look commits me to fresh debt,
And to pay little I must borrow yet ?
Enough of this already, now away !
With silent woods and hills untenanted
Let me go commune ; under thy sweet gloom,
O kind maternal darkness, hide my head :
The day may come I yet may re-assume
My place, and, these tired limbs recruited, seek
The task for which I now am all too weak.

IV.

Yes, I have lied, and so must walk my way,
Bearing the liar's curse upon my head ;
Letting my weak and sickly heart be fed
On food which does the present craving stay,

But may be clean denied me e'en to-day,
And though 'twere certain, yet were ought than bread;
Letting—for so they say, it seems, I said,
And I am all too weak to disobey !
Therefore for me sweet Nature's scenes reveal not
Their charm ; sweet Music greets me and I feel not ;
Sweet eyes pass off me uninspired ; yea, more,
The golden tide of opportunity
Flows wafting in friendships and better,—I
Unseeing, listless, pace along the shore.

v.

How often sit I, posing o'er
  My strange distorted youth,
Seeking in vain, in all my store,
  One feeling based on truth ;
Amid the maze of petty life
  A clue whereby to move,
A spot whereon in toil and strife
  To dare to rest and love.

So constant as my heart would be,
  Sô fickle as it must,
'Twere well for others as for me
  'Twere dry as summer dust.
Excitements come, and act and speech
  Flow freely forth;—but no,
Nor they, nor ought beside can reach
  The buried world below.

VI.

——Like a child
In some strange garden left awhile alone,
I pace about the pathways of the world,
Plucking light hopes and joys from every stem,
With qualms of vague misgivings in my heart
That payment at the last will be required,—
Payment I cannot make,—or guilt incurred,
And shame to be endured.

VII.

——Roused by importunate knocks
I rose, I turned the key, and let them in,
First one, anon another, and at length
In troops they came; for how could I, who once
Had let in one, nor looked him in the face,
Show scruples e'er again? So in they came,
A noisy band of revellers,—vain hopes,
Wild fancies, fitful joys; and there they sit
In my heart's holy place, and through the night
Carouse, to leave it when the cold grey dawn
Gleams from the East, to tell me that the time
For watching and for thought bestowed is gone.

VIII.

O kind protecting Darkness! as a child
Flies back to bury in his mother's lap

His shame and his confusion, so to thee,
O Mother Night, come I ! within the folds
Of thy dark robe hide thou me close; for I
So long, so heedless, with external things
Have played the liar, that whate'er I see,
E'en these white glimmering curtains, yon bright stars,
Which to the rest rain comfort down, for me
Smiling those smiles which I may not return,
Or frowning frowns of fierce triumphant malice,
As angry claimants or expectants sure
Of that I promised and may not perform,
Look me in the face !   O hide me, Mother Night !

IX.

Once more the wonted road I tread,
Once more dark heavens above me spread,
Upon the windy down I stand,
My station, whence the circling land
Lies mapped and pictured wide below;—
Such as it was, such e'en again,
Long dreary bank, and breadth of plain
By hedge or tree unbroken ;—lo,
A few green woods can only show
How vain their aid, and in the sense
Of one unaltering impotence,
Relieving not, meseems enhance
The sovereign dulness of the expanse.
Yet marks where human hand hath been,
Bare house, unsheltered village, space

Of ploughed and fenceless tilth between
(Such aspect as methinks may be
In some half-settled colony),
From nature vindicate the scene ;
A wide and yet disheartening view,
A melancholy world.
                  'Tis true,
Most true ; and yet, like those strange smiles
By fervent hope or tender thought
From distant happy regions brought,
Which upon some sick bed are seen
To glorify a pale worn face
With sudden beauty,—so at whiles
Lights have descended, hues have been,
To clothe with half-celestial grace
The bareness of the desert place.

   Since so it is, so be it still !
Could only thou, my heart, be taught
To treasure, and in act fulfil
The lesson which the sight has brought ;
In thine own dull and dreary state
To work and patiently to wait :
Little thou think'st in thy despair
How soon the o'ershaded sun may shine,
And e'en the dulling clouds combine
To bless with lights and hues divine
That region desolate and bare,
Those sad and sinful thoughts of thine !

Still doth the coward heart complain ;
The hour may come and come in vain ;
The branch that withered lies and dead
No suns can force to lift its head.
True !—yet how little thou canst tell
How much in thee is ill or well ;
Nor for thy neighbours, nor for thee,
Be sure, was life designed to be
A draught of dull complacency.
One Power too is it, who doth give
The food within us, and within
The strength that makes it nutritive :
He bids the dry bones rise and live,
And e'en in hearts depraved to sin
Some sudden gracious influence,
May give the long-lost good again,
And wake within the dormant sense
And love of good ;—for mortal men,
So but thou strive, thou soon shalt see
Defeat itself is victory.

So be it : yet : O Good and Great,
In whom in this bedarkened state
I fain am struggling to believe,
Let me not ever cease to grieve,
Nor lose the consciousness of ill
Within me ;—and refusing still
To recognise in things around
What cannot truly there be found,

Let me not feel, nor be it true,
That while each daily task I do
I still am giving day by day
My precious things within away,
(Those Thou didst give to keep as thine)
And casting, do whate'er I may,
My heavenly pearls to earthly swine.

X.

I have seen higher, holier things than these,
 And therefore must to these refuse my heart,
Yet am I panting for a little ease ;
 I'll take, and so depart.

Ah hold ! the heart is prone to fall away,
 Her high and cherished visions to forget,
And if thou takest, how wilt thou repay
 So vast, so dread a debt ?

How will the heart, which now thou trustest, then
 Corrupt, yet in corruption mindful yet,
Turn with sharp stings upon itself !   Again,
 Bethink thee of the debt !

—Hast thou seen higher, holier things than these,
 And therefore must to these thy heart refuse ?
With the true best, alack, how ill agrees
 The best that thou wouldst choose !

The Summum Pulchrum rests in heaven above;
Do thou, as best thou may'st, thy duty do:
Amid the things allowed thee live and love;
Some day thou shalt it view.

QUA CURSUM VENTUS.

As ships becalmed at eve, that lay
  With canvas drooping, side by side,
Two towers of sail at dawn of day
  Are scarce long leagues apart descried;

When fell the night, upsprung the breeze,
  And all the darkling hours they plied,
Nor dreamt but each the self-same seas
  By each was cleaving, side by side :

E'en so—but why the tale reveal
  Of those whom, year by year unchanged,
Brief absence joined anew to feel,
  Astounded, soul from soul estranged.

At dead of night their sails were filled,
  And onward each rejoicing steered—
Ah, neither blame, for neither willed,
  Or wist, what first with dawn appeared !

To veer, how vain ! On, onward strain,
  Brave barks ! In light, in darkness too,
Through winds and tides one compass guides—
  To that, and your own selves, be true.

But O blithe breeze ! and O great seas
    Though ne'er, that earliest parting past,
On your wide plain they join again,
    Together lead them home at last.

One port, methought, alike they sought,
    One purpose hold where'er they fare,—
O bounding breeze, O rushing seas,
    At last, at last, unite them there !

ALCAICS.

So spake the Voice; and, as with a single life
Instinct, the whole mass, fierce, irretainable,
    Down on that unsuspecting host swept
    Down, with the fury of winds that all night
Up-brimming, sapping slowly the dyke, at dawn
Full through the breach, o'er homestead, and harvest, and
    Herd roll a deluge; while the milkmaid
    Trips i' the dew, and remissly guiding
Morn's first uneven furrow, the farmer's boy
Dreams out his dream: so over the multitude
    Safe-tented, uncontrolled and uncon-
    Trollably sped the Avenger's fury.

NATURA NATURANS.

Beside me,—in the car,—she sat,
　She spake not, no, nor looked to me :
From her to me, from me to her,
　What passed so subtly, stealthily ?
As rose to rose that by it blows
　Its interchanged aroma

Beside me, naught but this—but this !
　That influent as within me dwelt
Her life, mine too within her breast,
　Her brain, her every limb she felt :
We sat; while o'er and in us, more
　And more, a power unknown prevailed,
Inhaling, and inhaled,—and still
　'Twas one, inhaling or inhaled.

Beside me, nought but this ;—and passed ;
　I passed; and know not to this day
If gold or jet her girlish hair,
　If black, or brown, or lucid-grey
Her eye's young glance : the fickle chance
　That joined us, yet may join again ;
But I no face again could greet
　As her's, whose life was in me then.

As unsuspecting mere a maid
  As, fresh in maidhood's bloomiest bloom,
In casual second-class did e'er
  By casual youth her seat assume ;
Or vestal, say, of saintliest clay,
  For once by balmiest airs betrayed
Unto emotions too, too sweet
  To be unlingeringly gainsaid :

Unowning then, confusing soon
  With dreamier dreams that o'er the glass
Of shyly ripening woman-sense
  Reflected, scarce reflected, pass,
A wife may-be, a mother she
  In Hymen's shrine recalls not now,
She first in hour, ah, not profane,
  With me to Hymen learnt to bow.

Ah no !—Yet owned we, fused in one,
  The Power which e'en in stones and earths
By blind elections felt, in forms
  Organic breeds to myriad births ;
By lichen small on granite wall
  Approved, its faintest feeblest stir
Slow-spreading, strengthening long, at last
  Vibrated full in me and her.

In me and her—sensation strange !
　The lily grew to pendent head,
To vernal airs the mossy bank
　Its sheeny primrose spangles spread,
In roof o'er roof of shade sun-proof
　Did cedar strong itself outclimb,
And altitude of aloe proud
　Aspire in floreal crown sublime ;

Flashed flickering forth fantastic flies,
　Big bees their burly bodies swung,
Rooks roused with civic din the elms,
　And lark its wild reveillez rung ;
In Libyan dell the light gazelle,
　The leopard lithe in Indian glade,
And dolphin, brightening tropic seas,
　In us were living, leapt and played:

　　　:

Their shells did slow crustacea build,
　Their gilded skins did snakes renew,
While mightier spines for loftier kind
　Their types in amplest limbs outgrew ;
Yea, close comprest in human breast,
　What moss, and tree, and livelier thing,
What Earth, Sun, Star of force possest,
　Lay budding, burgeoning forth for Spring.

Such sweet preluding sense of old
  Led on in Eden's sinless place
The hour when bodies human first
  Combined the primal prime embrace,
Such genial heat the blissful seat
  In man and woman owned unblamed,
When, naked both, its garden paths
  They walked unconscious, unashamed:

Ere, clouded yet in mistiest dawn,
  Above the horizon dusk and dun,
One mountain crest with light had tipped
  That Orb that is the Spirit's Sun;
Ere dreamed young flowers in vernal showers
  Of fruit to rise the flower above,
Or ever yet to young Desire
  Was told the mystic name of Love.

'Ο Θεὸς μετὰ σοῦ.*

FAREWELL, my Highland lassie ! when the year returns
    around,
Be it Greece, or be it Norway, where my vagrant feet are
    found,
I shall call to mind the place, I shall call to mind the day,
The day that's gone for ever, and the glen that's far
    away ;
I shall mind me,' be it Rhine or Rhone, Italian land or
    France,
Of the laughings, and the whispers, of the pipings and
    the dance ;
I shall see thy soft brown eyes dilate to wakening woman
    thought,
And whiter still the white cheek grow, to which the blush
    was brought ;
And oh, with mine commixing, I thy breath of life shall
    feel,
And clasp the shyly passive hands in joyous Highland
    reel ;
I shall hear, and see, and feel, and in sequence sadly
    true,
Shall repeat the bitter-sweet of the lingering last adieu ;
I shall seem as now to leave thee, with the kiss upon the
    brow,
And the fervent benediction of—ὁ Θεὸς μετὰ σοῦ !

* "God be with you."

Ah me, my Highland lassie ! though in winter drear and
    long
Deep arose the heavy snows, and the stormy winds were
    strong,
Though the rain, in summer's brightest, it were raining
    every day,
With worldly comforts few and far, how glad were I to
    stay !
I fall to sleep with dreams of life in some black bothie
    spent,
Coarse poortith's ware thou changing there to gold of
    pure content,
With barefoot lads and lassies round, and thee the cheery
    wife,
In the braes of old Lochaber a laborious homely life ;
But I wake—to leave thee, smiling, with the kiss upon
    the brow,
And the peaceful benediction of—ὁ Θεὸς μετὰ σοῦ !

.   .   .   .

ἐπὶ Λάτμῳ.

On the mountain, in the woodland,
In the shaded secret dell,
   I have seen thee, I have met thee!
In the soft ambrosial hours of night,
In darkness silent sweet
   I beheld thee, I was with thee,
   I was thine, and thou wert mine!

When I gazed in palace chambers,
When I trod the rustic dance,
Earthly maids were fair to look on,
Earthly maidens' hearts were kind:
Fair to look on, fair to love:
But the life, the life to me,
'Twas the death, the death to them,
In the spying, prying, prating,
Of a curious cruel world.
At a touch, a breath, they fade,
They languish, droop, and die;
Yea, the juices change to sourness,
And the tints to clammy brown;
And the softness unto foulness,
And the odour unto stench.

Let alone and leave to bloom;
Pass aside, nor make to die,
—In the woodland, on the mountain,
Thou art mine, and I am thine.

So I passed.—Amid the uplands,
In the forest, as whose skirts
Pace unstartled, feed unfearing
Do the roe-deer and the red,
While I hungered, while I thirsted,
While the night was deepest dark,
Who was I, that thou shouldst meet me?
Who was I, thou didst not pass?
Who was I, that I should say to thee,
Thou art mine, and I am thine?

To the air from whence thou camest
Thou returnest, thou art gone;
Self-created, dis-created,
Re-created, ever fresh,
Ever young!—
As a lake its mirrored mountains
At a moment, unregretting,
Unresisting, unreclaiming,
Without preface, without question,
On the silent shifting levels
Let's depart,
Shews, effaces and replaces!

For what is, anon is not ;
What has been, again's to be ;
Ever new and ever young,
Thou art mine, and I am thine.

Art thou she that walks the skies,
That rides the starry night ?
I know not——
For my meanness dares not claim the truth,
My loveliness declares.
But the face thou shew'st the world, is not
The face thou shew'st to me.
And the look that I have looked in
Is of none but me beheld.
I know not ; but I know
I am thine, and thou art mine.

And I watch : the orb behind
As it fleeteth, faint and fair
In the depth of azure night,
In the violet blank, I trace
By an outline, faint and fair
Her whom none but I beheld.
By her orb she moveth slow,
Graceful-slow, serenely firm,
Maiden-Goddess ! while her robe
The adoring planets kiss.
And I too cower and ask,
Wert thou mine, and was I thine ?

Hath a cloud o'ercast the sky?
Is it cloud upon the mountain-sides
Or haze of dewy river-banks
Below?—
Or around me,
To enfold me, to conceal,
Doth a mystic magic veil,
A celestial separation,
As of curtains hymeneal,
Undiscerned, yet all excluding,
Interpose?
For the pine-tree boles are dimmer,
And the stars undimmed above ;
In perspective brief, uncertain,
Are the forest alleys closed,
And to whispers indistinctest
The resounding torrents lulled.
Can it be and can it be?
Upon earth and here below,
In the woodlands at my side
Thou art with me, thou art here.

'Twas the vapour of the perfume
Of the presence that should be
That enwrapt me,
That enwraps us,
O my Goddess, O my Queen !
And I turn,
At thy feet to fall before thee,

And thou wilt not ;
At thy feet to kneel, and reach, and kiss thy finger-tips,
And thou wilt not,
And I feel thine arms that stay me,
And I feel——
O mine own, mine own, mine own,
I am thine, and thou art mine !

"IF, WHEN IN CHEERLESS WANDERINGS."

IF, when in cheerless wanderings, dull and cold,
A sense of human kindliness hath found us,
　　We seem to have around us
　　An atmosphere all gold,
'Mid darkest shades a halo rich of shine,
An element, that while the bleak wind bloweth,
　　On the rich heart bestoweth
　　Inbreathed draughts of wine ;
Heaven guide, the cup be not, as chance may be,
To some vain mate given up as soon as tasted !
　　No, nor on thee be wasted,
　　Thou trifler, Poesy !
Heaven grant the manlier heart, that timely, ere
Youth fly, with life's real tempest would be coping:
　　The fruit of dreamy hoping
　　Is, waking, blank despair.

"IS IT TRUE, YE GODS?"

Is it true, ye gods, who treat us
As the gambling fool is treated,
O ye, who ever cheat us,
And let us feel we're cheated !
Is it true that poetical power,
The gift of Heaven, the dower
Of Apollo and the Nine,
The inborn sense, "the vision and the faculty
    divine,"
All we glorify and bless
In our rapturous exaltation,
All invention, and creation,
Exuberance of fancy, and sublime imagination,
All a poet's fame is built on,
The fame of Shakespeare, Milton,
Of Wordsworth, Byron, Shelley,
Is in reason's grave precision,
Nothing more, nothing less,
Than a peculiar conformation,
Constitution and condition
Of the brain and of the belly ?
Is it true, ye gods, who cheat us ?
And that's the way ye treat us ?

O say it, all who think it,
Look straight, and never blink it !

If it is so, let it be so,
And we will all agree so;
But the plot has counter plot,
It may be, and yet be not.

UPON THE WATER.*

Upon the water in a boat,
I sit and sketch, as there we float;
The scene is fair, the stream is strong,
I sketch it as we float along.

The stream is strong, and as I sit
And view the picture that we quit,
It flows and flows, and bears the boat,
And I sit sketching as we float.

Still as we go, the things I see,
E'en as I see them, cease to be,
The angles shift, and with the boat
The whole perspective seems to float.

Each pointed height, each wavy line,
To new and other forms combine;
Proportions change and colours fade,
And all the landscape is remade.

Depicted—neither far nor near,
And larger there and smaller here,
And partly old, and partly new,
E'en I can hardly think it true.

* From the "Letters of Parepidemus" (1853).

UPON THE WATER.

Yet still I look, and still I sit,
Adjusting, shaping, altering it ;
And still the current bears the boat
And me, still sketching as we float.

"IN VAIN I SEEM TO CALL." *

In vain I seem to call, and yet
Think not the living years forget :
Ages of heroes fought and fell,
That Homer, in the end, might tell :
O'er grovelling generations past
The Doric column rose at last.
A thousand hearts on thousand years
Had wasted labour, hopes, and fears,
Knells, laughters, and unmeaning tears,
Ere England's Shakespeare saw, or Rome,
The pure perfection of her dome.
Others, I doubt not, if not we,
The issue of our toils shall see;
Young children gather as their own
The harvest that the Dead have sown —
The Dead, forgotten and unknown.

* From the "Letters of Parepidemus" (1853).

WALTER SCOTT PRESS, FELLING, NEWCASTLE-ON-TYNE.

COMPACT AND PRACTICAL.

In Limp Cloth; for the Pocket.   Price One Shilling.

THE EUROPEAN
CONVERSATION BOOKS.

FRENCH.   **ITALIAN.**

SPANISH.   **GERMAN.**

NORWEGIAN.

CONTENTS.

Hints to Travellers—Everyday Expressions—Arriving at and Leaving a Railway Station — Custom House Enquiries—In a Train—At a Buffet and Restaurant— At an Hotel—Paying an Hotel Bill—Enquiries in a Town—On Board Ship—Embarking and Disembarking —Excursion by Carriage—Enquiries as to Diligences— Enquiries as to Boats—Engaging Apartments—Washing List and Days of Week — Restaurant Vocabulary — Telegrams and Letters, etc., etc.

The contents of these little handbooks are so arranged as to permit direct and immediate reference. All dialogues or enquiries not considered absolutely essential have been purposely excluded, nothing being introduced which might confuse the traveller rather than assist him. A few hints are given in the introduction which will be found valuable to those unaccustomed to foreign travel.

London · WALTER SCOTT, LIMITED, Paternoster Square.

LIBRARY OF HUMOUR.

Cloth Elegant, Large Crown 8vo.   Price 3/6 each.

VOLUMES ALREADY ISSUED.

THE HUMOUR OF FRANCE. Translated, with an Introduction and Notes, by Elizabeth Lee. With numerous
Illustrations by Paul Frénzeny.

THE HUMOUR OF GERMANY. Translated, with an Introduction and Notes, by Hans Müller-Casenov. With
numerous Illustrations by C. E. Brock.

THE HUMOUR OF ITALY. Translated, with an Introduction and Notes, by A. Werner. With 50 Illustrations by
Arturo Faldi.

THE HUMOUR OF AMERICA. Edited, with an Introduction and Notes, by J. Barr (of the *Detroit Free Press*).
With numerous Illustrations by C. E. Brock.

THE HUMOUR OF HOLLAND. Translated, with an Introduction and Notes, by A. Werner. With numerous Illustrations by Dudley Hardy.

THE HUMOUR OF IRELAND. Selected by D. J.
O'Donoghue. With numerous Illustrations by Oliver
Paque.

THE HUMOUR OF SPAIN. Translated, with an Introduction and Notes, by S. Taylor. With numerous Illustrations
by H. R. Millar.

THE HUMOUR OF RUSSIA. Translated, with Notes, by
E. L. Boole, and an Introduction by Stepniak. With 50
Illustrations by Paul Frénzeny.

IN PREPARATION.

THE HUMOUR OF JAPAN. Translated, with an Introduction, by A. M. With Illustrations by George Bigot (from
Drawings made in Japan).

London: WALTER SCOTT, LIMITED, Paternoster Square.

THE CANTERBURY POETS.

EDITED BY WILLIAM SHARP.   1/- VOLS., SQUARE 8VO.

PHOTOGRAVURE EDITION, 2/-.

London: WALTER SCOTT, Paternoster Square.

THE SCOTT LIBRARY.

Cloth, uncut edges, gilt top.   Price 1/6 per volume.

Political Orations.
Holmes's Autocrat.
Holmes's Poet.
Holmes's Professor.
Chesterfield's Letters.
Stories from Carleton.
Jane Eyre.
Elizabethan England.
Davis's Writings.
Spence's Anecdotes.
More's Utopia.
Sadi's Gulistan.
English Folk Tales.
Northern Studies.
Famous Reviews.
Aristotle's Ethics.
Landor's Aspasia.
Tacitus.
Essays of Elia.
Balzac.
De Musset's Comedies.
Darwin's Coral-Reefs.
Sheridan's Plays.
Our Village.
Humphrey's Clock, &c.
Tales from Wonderland.
Douglas Jerrold.
Rights of Woman.
Athenian Oracle.
Essays of Sainte-Beuve.
Selections from Plato.
Heine's Travel Sketches.
Maid of Orleans.
Sydney Smith.
The New Spirit.
Marvellous Adventures.
    (From the Morte d'Arthur.)
Helps's Essays.

Montaigne's Essays.
Luck of Barry Lyndon
William Tell.
Carlyle's German Essays
Lamb's Essays.
Wordsworth's Prose.
Leopardi's Dialogues.
Inspector-General (Gogol).
Bacon's Essays.
Prose of Milton.
Plato's Republic.
Passages from Froissart.
Prose of Coleridge.
Heine in Art and Letters.
Essays of De Quincey.
Vasari's Lives.
The Laocoon.
Plays of Maeterlinck.
Walton's Angler.
Lessing's Nathan the Wise
Renan's Essays.
Goethe's Maxims.
Schopenhauer's Essays.
Renan's Life of Jesus.
Confessions of St. Augustine.
Principles of Success in
    Literature (G. H. Lewes)
What is Art? (Tolstoy)
Walton's Lives
Renan's Antichrist
Orations of Cicero.
Reflections on the Revolution in France (Burke).
Letters of the Younger
    Pliny. 2 vols., 1st and 2nd
    Series.
Selected Thoughts of
    Blaise Pascal.

New Series of Critical Biographies.

Edited by ERIC ROBERTSON and FRANK T. MARZIALS.

GREAT WRITERS.

Cloth, Gilt Top, Price 1s. 6d.

ALREADY ISSUED—

GREAT WRITERS—*continued.*

LIFE OF CRABBE. By T. E. KEBBEL, M.A.

LIFE OF HEINE. By WILLIAM SHARP.

LIFE OF MILL. By W. L. COURTNEY.

LIFE OF SCHILLER. By H. W. NEVINSON.

LIFE OF CAPTAIN MARRYAT. By DAVID HANNAY.

LIFE OF LESSING. By T. W. ROLLESTON.

LIFE OF MILTON. By RICHARD GARNETT.

LIFE OF GEORGE ELIOT. By OSCAR BROWNING.

LIFE OF BALZAC. By FREDERICK WEDMORE.

LIFE OF JANE AUSTEN. By GOLDWIN SMITH.

LIFE OF BROWNING. By WILLIAM SHARP.

LIFE OF BYRON. By Hon. RODEN NOEL.

LIFE OF HAWTHORNE. By MONCURE CONWAY.

LIFF OF SCHOPENHAUER. By Professor WALLACE.

LIFE OF SHERIDAN. By LLOYD SANDERS.

LIFE OF THACKERAY. By HERMAN MERIVALE and FRANK T. MARZIALS.

LIFE OF CERVANTES. By H. E. WATTS.

LIFE OF VOLTAIRE. By FRANCIS ESPINASSE.

LIFE OF LEIGH HUNT. By COSMO MONKHOUSE.

LIFE OF WHITTIER. By W. J. LINTON.

LIFE OF RENAN. By FRANCIS ESPINASSE.

LIFE OF THOREAU. By H. S. SALT.

Bibliography to each, by J. P. ANDERSON, British Museum.

LIBRARY EDITION OF "GREAT WRITERS."

Printed on large paper of extra quality, in handsome binding, Demy 8vo, price 2s. 6d. per volume.

London: WALTER SCOTT, Paternoster Square.

Crown 8vo, Cloth Elegant, in Box, Price 2s. 6d.

THE CULT OF BEAUTY:

A MANUAL OF PERSONAL HYGIENE.

By C. J. S. THOMPSON.

CONTENTS—

"'Quackery,' says Mr. Thompson, 'was never more rampant than it is to-day' with regard to 'aids in beautifying the person.' His little book is based on purely hygienic principles, and comprises recipes for toilet purposes which he warrants are 'practical and harmless.' These are virtues in any book of health and beauty, and Mr. Thompson's advice and guidance are, we find, not wanting in soundness and common-sense."— *Saturday Review.*

London : WALTER SCOTT, Paternoster Square.

1/- Booklets by Count Tolstoy.

Bound in White Grained Boards, with Gilt Lettering.

WHERE LOVE IS, THERE GOD IS ALSO.
THE TWO PILGRIMS.
WHAT MEN LIVE BY.   THE GODSON.
IF YOU NEGLECT THE FIRE, YOU DON'T PUT IT OUT.
WHAT SHALL IT PROFIT A MAN?

2/- Booklets by Count Tolstoy.

NEW EDITIONS, REVISED.

Small 12mo, Cloth, with Embossed Design on Cover, each
containing Two Stories by Count Tolstoy, and Two
Drawings by H. R. Millar.   In Box, Price 2s. each.

Volume I. contains—
WHERE LOVE IS, THERE GOD IS ALSO.
THE GODSON.
Volume II. contains—
WHAT MEN LIVE BY.
WHAT SHALL IT PROFIT A MAN?
Volume III. contains—
THE TWO PILGRIMS.
IF YOU NEGLECT THE FIRE, YOU DON'T PUT IT OUT.
Volume IV. contains—
MASTER AND MAN.
Volume V. contains—
TOLSTOY'S PARABLES.

London : WALTER SCOTT, Paternoster Square,

" The most attractive Birthday Book ever published."
Crown Quarto, in specially designed Cover, Cloth, Price 6s.
" Wedding Present " Edition, in Silver Cloth, 7s. 6d., in Box.
Also in Limp Morocco, in Box.

An Entirely New Edition.   Revised Throughout.

With Twelve Full-Page Portraits of Celebrated Musicians.

DEDICATED TO PADEREWSKI.

THE MUSIC OF THE POETS.

A MUSICIANS' BIRTHDAY BOOK.

COMPILED BY ELEONORE D'ESTERRE-KEELING.

THIS is an entirely new edition of this popular work.   A special feature of the book consists in the reproduction in fac-simile of autographs, and autographic music, of living composers ; among the many new autographs which have been added to the present edition being those of MM. Paderewski (to whom the book is dedicated), Mascagni, Eugen d' Albert, Sarasate, Hamish McCunn, and C. Hubert Parry.   Merely as a volume of poetry about music, this book makes a charming anthology, the selections of verse extending from a period anterior to Chaucer to the present day.   A new binding has also been specially designed.

London : WALTER SCOTT, Paternoster Square.